Yes, M'Lady

'People are willing to give their right arms to be caricatured in Spitting Image. *Even though the portrayal may be cynical, even down right cruel, somehow it is flattering to be thought important enough to be "puppeteered" in this way.*

Thunderbirds *was way ahead of its time. Although in no way cynical and only intended as sci-fi fun, the puppets were surely forerunners of today's high-tech wizardry.*

It was great to be part of something so innovative and successful.'

CLIFF RICHARD, 1991

'It was a toss up whether I married Lady Penelope or Jackie [his long-time wife]. I was upset that I wasn't asked to play any puppet characters!'

ADAM FAITH, 1991

'I was thrilled when I was asked to play voices in Thunderbirds. *I was a great fan.'*

BOB MONKHOUSE, 1991

'Just tell us about Thunderbirds *– how was it made? – and about Lady Penelope. We loved the series.'*

THE ROLLING STONES, PARIS, 1978

Yes, M'Lady

Sylvia
Anderson

SMITH GRYPHON
PUBLISHERS

First published in Great Britain in 1991 by
SMITH GRYPHON LIMITED
Swallow House, 11-21 Northdown Street
London N1 9BN

First impression November 1991
Second impression November 1991

Designed by Hammond Hammond

A CIP catalogue record for this book
is available from the British Library

ISBN 1 85685 011 0

Typeset by
Computerset, Harmondsworth, Middlesex
Printed in Great Britain by
The Bath Press, Avon

DEDICATION

Over the years, much has been written about the *Thunderbirds* phenomenon. However, little has been said about the team of talented people behind the scenes. While this book is my personal story and, therefore, told from my perspective, it would be impossible for me not to mention the people who contributed to that success story, not least, Lew Grade, who believed in us and made it all possible. It is to him and the team that this book is dedicated

CONTENTS

FOREWORD

Of all the stars with whom I was involved during my career, Lady Penelope – as created and played by Sylvia Anderson – was one of my favourites.

She was never temperamental, was never late on the set and never drove me crazy with excessive demands for an elaborate wardrobe or expensive holidays. In spite of this, she always looked gorgeous, always wore the most glamorous clothes and was never seen without her pink Rolls-Royce with the famous FAB 1 number plate, impeccably driven by the chauffeur, Parker.

Those early days of *Thunderbirds* bring back very happy memories. The animation field was a totally new experience for me and, as each series developed, I became more and more fascinated by the originality of the stunning visual effects – so prophetically in advance of their time – as well as with the lifelike process of Supermarionation.

LORD GRADE OF ELSTREE

ACKNOWLEDGMENTS

My thanks to Jonathan Keeble for his invaluable help in researching this book. Also to Derek Meddings, John Read, Mary Turner, John Brown and others for their recollections; to Sandra Pope for helping me to meet a deadline by typing all hours, Clive Carr, and Helen Armitage for meticulous editing. To Keith Shackleton for his encouragement and memory jogging, Jeannie Sakol, my long-time New York friend for effecting the right introduction, Robert Smith for his recognition of the potential and to loyal friends like Ann Cotton and my family for just being there. And a special thank you to my son for suggesting that I write the book in the first place. And for all those who have supported and believed in me during the 'solo' years, not the least, my dear friend Michael Fuchs.

The author and publishers would like to thank *New Scientist* and the *Daily Mirror* for permission to reproduce extracts on pp. 31-3 and pp. 46-7.

1

HOW IT ALL BEGAN

I took one last look at the Empire State Building – majestic in its New York street. Now devoid of activity – it was silent and doomed. The atmosphere was tense, nerves frayed as someone hissed a warning not to speak. The experts put the finishing touches to their strategically placed explosive charges and there was an air of conspiracy: much rode on this moment and as the countdown continued relentlessly there was no turning back. Soon we would know if the weeks of elaborate preparation were going to pay off.

Suddenly there was an ear-splitting explosion and I watched with fascination as the world-famous triumph of architecture disintegrated into a million fragments and was gone for ever. We all heaved a sigh of relief: Mission Accomplished. All we had to do now was to cut and print. It was true, we had blown up the Empire State Building: perfect in every detail, a work of art, but only 18 inches high! This was, of course, a scene from one of the *Thunderbirds* episodes. In our miniature world just about anything could happen and usually did, both in front and behind the camera.

I wandered off the shooting-stage, congratulating Derek Meddings, our brilliant visual effects director, on yet another lifelike model shot. As I walked past the row of cutting-rooms, I smiled to myself at the disjointed snatches of dialogue that echoed along the corridor from the moviolas. I headed towards my office and was met by my secretary with an urgent problem on Stage 4: could I get there right away? Almost simultaneously my bleeper wailed and I returned Lew Grade's call, reassuring him that Lady Penelope would not be too posh for the American market. Yes, they would understand her accent; I'd played the voice as classlessly as possible without losing the ladylike quality. Reassured, Lew Grade wished us luck with the new series. He had financed and sponsored us, had steered us through since the early days, but, more importantly, he had believed in us and given us our head creatively. His phone call was a rare event and I made a note of his concerns.

The trouble on Stage 4 proved to be an elaborate hairstyle that prevented the head from rotating. My role was to placate a weary director and quickly organize a more simple hair-do so that filming could continue. On arrival back at my office, through the busy complex that made up our puppet studios on the most unHollywood-like site of the Slough trading-estate, I passed some of the 150 people we employed in our busy Disney-type mini studio. The company now embraced a whole host of by-products, such as toys, publishing and fashions, with subsidiary companies fast growing to meet the demands of an ever avid public. I sank into a seat behind my desk in its plush ultra-modern setting and closed my eyes: how had I become involved in this Lilliput of the film world?

As long as I can remember I had been fascinated by the world of make-believe. I had been brought up in a show-business atmosphere in as much as my father was a boxing promoter and ran his own gymnasium in south London. As a small child I had met all the stars of the ring and was very spoilt by these gentle giants when I visited my father in his office. There I made phone calls and scribbled notes on pieces of paper, pretending to be a busy and important person. I could only have been about four years old, but I remember it clearly. There was an air of excitement when a boxing show was being arranged and our family fortunes varied greatly on the success or failure of the venture. As a promoter, my father would sink everything he had into the shows – there were no half measures. As an ex-fighter himself, he understood the rough justice of the boxing world and his stories were – and still are – fascinating to me.

I think the precarious life-style of my childhood prepared me for my career to come, though I did not always appreciate my father's comment that, 'Each day in life is like stepping into the boxing ring.' As a rather snobbish and romantic teenager, I thought such a philosophy rather less than poetic. I preferred Shakespeare's version: 'All the world's a stage,' but I guess when you pare life down it comes to the same thing!

Born with the unusual name of Beatrice Aberdeen, doubtless of Scottish origin, my mother was the eloquent one of the family and had a way with words. Pretty and artistic, she began training as a court dressmaker but found the job tedious. She could design and make any outfit she chose and as a child I was used to a different outfit each week effortlessly run up by my mother. This combination of both my parents personalities and their respective talents gave me a lively heritage for which I am now grateful.

Our bi-weekly visits to the cinema were the highlight of my life and I knew every movie star and their films off by heart. I often went to the theatre with Nan, my maternal grandmother, and a particularly vivid memory remains of meeting the cast of *Cinderella* when we were having tea in the little café by the theatre after the show. It was then, aged five, that I knew I had to be involved in show business and my fascination was formed by my mother's two cousins who were working on the halls and were protégés of the legendary Ellen Terry. Their visits to us, when they sang and played the piano, were magic to me.

Thus inspired, I took piano and singing lessons, from a rather large woman whose home always smelled of overcooked cabbage, and danced with The Terry Juveniles, a child dancing-troupe. Later I staged my own show in our back garden with my sister, Betty, playing the star role. I, of course, produced and directed it, and rehearsed my cast as hard as if they were preparing for a West End first night. When I was only ten, I even auditioned for a musical. My parents were horrified though, and did not quite believe me until a card came through the post asking me to re-audition when I was fourteen. So the stage was set long ago for my involvement with my eventual career. However, before that time, I had settled down to some hard academic work.

As the leading light in amateur dramatics at school and winner of the school prize for journalism, in retrospect it appears inevitable that I should get involved with the arts in some shape or form; I eventually, of course, became fascinated with film-making. But before this my head-mistress, a formidable lady and sister of the Second World War hero, Orde Wingate, encouraged me to take the more sober path of reading economics and sociology at university. While I enjoyed my days at the

London School of Economics tremendously and, indeed, still retain a great interest in politics and world affairs, my real love was still the arts. So, after university when I saw an advertisement in a local newspaper for a part-time secretary with a small film company, I leaped at the opportunity.

It was a hot summer's day in 1957 as I trudged up a steep hill and cursed myself for wearing a suit. It was not the first time I had tried to break in to the film world – previously I had trekked Wardour Street, the heart of London filmland, in search of a job. Mostly, though, I had been greeted only by bored, overweight film types, whose sole interest in me was my youthful looks and the measure of my sex-appeal. But, ever the optimist, I made my way again to yet another interview, to keep, as it later turned out, a date with destiny.

Almost in despair of ever finding the country house that apparently doubled as a film studio, eventually I came across a lifeless, run-down building – its grounds neglected and overgrown – that looked like something out of a Hitchcock movie. I checked the name to ensure that I had the correct address; it was far from my mental picture of a bustling film studio. I encircled the house, trying several locked doors and when none of the bells elicited a response, my heart sank and I muttered to myself that it was yet another wasted effort. My instinct was to head back down the road and forget the whole thing: there was nothing inviting about this lonely country house, nothing even vaguely to suggest that this would prove to be the most momentous day of my life and the beginning of a new and exciting era.

Finally giving up hope of ever finding anyone at home, I turned to leave and, as I did so, caught sight of the shadowy figure of a man at one of the upper-storey windows. He motioned me to yet another hidden door and there I was ushered into a dingy, dark hallway. After brief introductions were made, I followed the small, bespectacled professor-type into a large and cold oak-panelled room. I was, by now, really feeling apprehensive and wishing I was anywhere but there. What had I stumbled upon? What sort of weird film-makers were these? Two younger men were perched behind a ridiculously large desk and seemed equally unreal. Nervously, they proceeded to interview me, although I had already decided to myself that I would turn down whatever they offered me. My chief interest was to make my excuses and escape as soon as possible.

During the course of the interview, I learned that the film company, Polytechnic, made documentaries and commercials. It was new and struggling, and could only afford to pay a small, part-time salary; I said I would consider their offer and we agreed to talk again in a few days. In any case, they had other people to interview. I heard myself joking about how they would be lucky if anyone else turned up for interview as the studio was so hard to find, but no one laughed. They were just very serious people, very earnest about their work, and somehow quite vulnerable. I do not know who was more nervous, them or me.

As I escaped finally and hurried out into the bright sunshine, I remember experiencing a small pang of compassion for these film-makers who were so obviously struggling. Resolutely I dismissed it from my mind. As far as I was concerned, the struggle was their own and for me it was the end of the episode; I doubted that I would hear from them again.

A week later, however, I received a frantic phone call from Polytechnic, asking if I could please start work at once. After much deliberation and many applications, they had decided to offer me the job at the fantastic part-time salary of £4 per week. I was made to feel that I had been bestowed the highest honour and remember thinking, 'What a cheek!', as I politely refused with the excuse that I had decided to accept a supply-teaching job. Suddenly, to my amazement, they dropped the façade and the voice at the other end of the line literally begged me to help them out. They'd just landed a commercial and were hopelessly disorganized; they needed someone to act as their Girl Friday, only for a few days. Somehow they succeeded in arousing my youthful, maternal instincts for adventure and compassion, and I found myself lamely accepting their meagre salary without a word of protest, even promising to start that very day.

I learned later that there had been some controversy over hiring me. One of the directors, who was not present at my interview, had argued strongly in favour of engaging a sensible, middle-aged lady with vast secretarial experience, whom he felt, quite correctly, would have just the right sobering influence. Not having met me, but with full reports of my youthful enthusiasm and lack of experience, he was, quite rightly, dubious about their choice. However, the vote was in my favour and Gerry Anderson reluctantly gave in. Thus some of the links in the chain were forged, and while later some new ones would be added, others, sadly, would be broken for good.

My initial fears about the film company were quite unfounded and the films they made were not blue, if you can discount a commercial for Blue Cap cheese. In their own ways, the five directors were all equally talented, mad, charming and infuriating. They each protected and overworked me in turn and my tasks were many and varied, ranging from elegant receptionist/secretary/personal assistant during VIP visits from prospective clients to tea girl/assistant cleaner/painter and decorator, even script girl and cashier (even though my petty cash never did balance out!). You name it, I did it, and loved every minute of it. Needless to say, my part-time job became a twelve-hour-a-day stint, earning me the enormous sum of £6.10s.0d. per week!

Soon I had my five bosses figured out: the most senior, and the founder, was a lovely, dreamy intellectual character with a highly creative mind, who rarely completed a single project, and was hopeless with money (everyone else's including his own), but who had infinite wisdom, charm and Welsh humour. It was he who had first appeared at the window and quite wrongly given the impression of being weird. Of the four other directors, only one was to play a vital part in my life and that was my future husband and business partner, Gerry Anderson, a tall, slim, earnest young man, who hero worshipped the senior partner, but had more in common with Arthur Provis, the brilliant team cameraman and fellow director.

These were happy days, even though there was never enough money to go round. The supply of work was insufficient to keep the company going, despite producing several advertising commercials and film titles. There were simply too many creative brains and egos to satisfy and, later in 1957, a breakaway group was formed. The five minds were to go two separate ways.

By now I had become very much a part of both the team and its dream, but I was particulary allied to Gerry and Arthur. They confided in me their plans to leave and form their own company, AP Films, and wondered if I would join them? They had also approached two members of the talented art department, John Read and Reg Hill. Sad as I was to see the original team break up, I was not surprised as I had mediated often in confrontations. I heard differing points of view – all sincere, all worthy – but to me there was only one group with which I felt in unison.

So, reluctantly, I bade one of the endless farewells that seem so inevitably part of life, to begin the second stage of my film career.

With the new company, AP Films (standing for Anderson and Provis), I assumed a new role as a company director. I had acquired knowledge of the film world that would prove invaluable there, but the only snag was that there was no work. We had rented an office in a beautiful country mansion by the river in Maidenhead, converting the ballroom into a shooting film stage. With a typewriter, a filing-cabinet (pitifully empty), a secondhand desk and a telephone, the sum total of our resources was around £500, including a £100 loan from my mother, the first of several. We were raring to go – eager and talented, but pitifully naïve – and we wanted to make a movie epic. What we finally landed – *The Adventures of Twizzle* – was very far removed from that. But at least it was work and we were delighted as our funds and morale had sunk dangerously low. Later we learned that we had only got the job because we had quoted a ridiculously low budget – much lower than any of the other small film companies.

The Adventures of Twizzle, and later, in 1959, *Torchy*, were based on stories by a writer of children's books, and with them we were launched into the world of puppetry. We did not all dote on puppets as children and have puppet theatres; the raw truth is that we needed the work and that was all there was on offer. The stories were straightforward and simple, and we shot them in front of a basic painted backdrop with puppets that were primitive, their movements jerky. It was the archetypical marionette production produced on a shoestring and it showed, but the series was made with great pride as the first production of AP Films. There was no way we could have known that this was to be the beginning of a long and ultimately highly successful television cult.

We were learning fast and began to realize that we could do our own complete productions in house: we could write the stories and film them in our own way. As the aspiring writer of the group, I began to script the stories, while Gerry directed, Reg Hill art directed and Arthur Provis and John Read operated the camera. We covered all the key roles of film-making and were firmly in business. There was one drawback though to our idyllic setting by the river. During the summer it was perfect, but in winter, when it flooded, we were virtually cut off from civilization and often had to ferry parts of the scenery to the main house. We did not have it easy in any other respect either. Puppet strings would break, unions descend on us for covering too many jobs, and while carpenters sawed in a corner, we attempted to give instructions on filming and play back the dialogue on tape. We could not afford full-time staff, so people would come in to work during the evenings, after their regular jobs, to paint scenery, build sets and models. We were underfunded and overworked.

By this time I was directing the dialogue as well as writing it and I have memories of hilarious recording sessions with Kenneth Connor, playing a multi-variety of voices, Denise Bryer and Nicholas Parsons (then husband and wife), and Jill Raymond (married to Clement Freud). Between productions I was farmed out to other companies, often 'temping' in dreary offices.

I assisted Gerry in the cutting-rooms when we landed a revoicing job on a Frankie Howerd film and was told that if I lost a piece of film I would have to stay until it was found. Gerry was a hard taskmaster, but I was eager to learn. Often our work took us late into the night and through the early hours of the morning; sometimes we never went home. Angry relatives resented being excluded from our world and while marriages went on the rocks, we were still on a roll, with no turning back. Broken romances, illness, family crises all came second to the survival of the company.

It was the pre-dawn of the sixties and we were laying the foundation for the success that awaited us. The timing was right; the opportunities just round the corner. The Beatles were limbering up for their launch; the permissive society was about to burst on the scene. There would be more hard times, but more work too.

Now that we were launched into the world of puppets we began to realize the advantages of our miniature stars and sets. Without life-size sets, without foreign locations, we could set our stories in virtually any place or time. So with the world literally at our feet, what could be more commercial than the ever popular western? In this climate of optimism *Four Feather Falls* was conceived, complete with the stereotyped characters that we had all been brought up with in Hollywood movies: the sheriff (Tex Tucker), Dan Morse of the telegraph office, Little Jake the boy hero, the singing horse, the villain, we had them all. The only character missing was the bar-room saloon's good-time gal, because after all, it was a programme for children's television.

We sold the idea to Granada television. On the strength of it we acquired the lease of a trading-estate factory warehouse and bought camera equipment and editing machines on hire-purchase. We were convinced that this was the end of our financial problems. The first series was a great success and we waited for the phone to ring, for Granada to order another series. After all we had the sets, the puppets, the equipment, the studio space, but nothing happened. Much debate followed about whether we should seem eager or whether we should stay cool, but slowly we realized that time was not on our side: there were hire-purchase payments to be made, rent and crew to be paid. Sadly, one by one, we had to let people go, until only the company directors remained.

We finally made the phone call to Granada, who said they would not be wanting any more shows. After all, they had a series, which they could always rescreen; to them it was only a kids' show and not worth further investment, a resource repeatable to successive generations of children. We were desperate now more than ever before, because for the first time we had everything to lose, and not just our hopes and ambitions. We had commitments and were mortgaged to the limit of our means.

Despondently we looked around at the studio we had come to regard as our own and started to consider subletting the lease. I cleaned out the toilets and tidied up the offices ready to show prospective tenants. Then I called an old friend and colleague, Frank Sherwin Green, who had given us work before when we had made film titles. He was a marvellous character, a real film-production man. Maybe he could find us individual jobs.

I confessed to Frank that we were on the verge of going out of business: could he put any business our way? Frank was shocked and insisted that we must not give up, that we had worked too hard to throw it all away. I tried to explain that we had no choice. Frank was adamant, however, that we should do nothing until he came round later that night. He was optimistic that there was a solution to our problems. Although I wanted to believe him, in my heart I doubted anything could be done, but I was willing to try. Frank was right: we had worked too hard, sacrificed too much to let it all go now.

That night we met Frank, and as we talked and drank a lot, even cried a little, he finally announced that there was someone we should meet: a friend of his, Connery Chapel, who knew Lew Grade. He felt that contacting Connery Chapel was a long shot but just might work. Maybe he could help. 'Who's Lew Grade?' I remember asking. Frank expressed surprise at my ignorance of the name of the man who was practically the boss of ATV.

So, there was, after all, a ray of hope and we clung to it like survivors of a shipwreck to a buoyant craft. But we were cautious: we had held high hopes before and were still broke, without work and in debt. This was the film business, however, and sometimes dreams really do come true. When, later that week, we did meet Lew Grade, we were more than fortunate that he recognized our potential and chose to back us all the way.

Lew asked us about our next project, and the truth was that we didn't have one, having thought only in terms of another series of *Four Feather Falls*. Still there was no way we were going to admit this, and as I had written some children's stories currently under consideration with Collins, the publishers, we asked them to return them to us at once and presented him with our next project: *Supercar*.

Before we knew it we were back in production: ordering materials, rehiring crew and committing ourselves to a lot of money. Still we had nothing in writing from Lew Grade and worried lest we were assuming too much without the security of a written contract. As we did not know Lew then, we dared to broach the subject with him and ask him for written confirmation of his verbal promise. He was furious and yelled at us that his word was the contract, and how right he was. After that we always got a signed contract, but often not until after we had started filming. He never once let us down, and so began the next phase of our film career leading up to *Thunderbirds*. From our involvement with Lew Grade, everything was set for success.

With the backing of ATV we were able to employ more staff and train young, enthusiastic technicians in our specialized line of work: young art students and stage puppeteers, sculptors, visual-effects trainees. Some of our early crew were still with us, now full time, like Derek Meddings, for example, who became involved with the design of the futuristic craft as well as painted backings. Reg Hill, one of the original directors, was in charge of these aspects, while John Read concentrated on the photographic side, and Gerry handled the direction and editing. I was involved with the scripts and the development of the characters.

We were now a very tight team covering most aspects of the production. Reg Hill and Gerry had come up with the idea of a car that could do anything – on land, on sea and in space. It was their schoolboy dream and thus the Supercar was born. I set to work on the characters and the storylines and this time I even played the part of our boy hero, Jimmy, as well as my usual repertoire of assorted voices. In one episode I remember playing the two main parts of Jimmy and Princess Caroline, when Jimmy and Supercar rescue the young Princess. The story was practically a two-hander with me talking to me. In order to change my voice from Jimmy to Caroline naturally I had to pause and every pause had to be edited out before the scene was played back to the puppeteers. I was now also editing voice tapes, which proved a nightmare. At that time there was no sophisticated splicing equipment, just a sharp edge and editing tape, a steady hand and lots and lots of patience.

Supercar was significant on many counts, not least in the creation of Supermarionation, a term coined to embrace all the techniques that had been developed by us and which were now incorporated into our filming. From the early days of *Twizzle* we had come quite a long way in a relatively short space of time: a special hair-like steel-tungsten wire was being developed that was less visible on camera; an electronic mouth movement had been devised so that the puppets reacted simultaneously to the voice tape, making obsolete the 'human' split-second delay as the puppet operators reacted to the recorded dialogue; and, to complete the illusion, back projection was used to create movement in the background for travelling shots. In many ways we were the pioneers of techniques that were to be used years later in some of the most sophisticated epic movies. This small team of artists and technicians beavering away on the Slough trading estate, under the umbrella of AP Films, was making film history.

Between 1957 and 1960, apart from our success in our miniature world, there was also significant movement in the real world. During the filming of *Supercar,* Gerry and I had taken time off to get married. As our work had intensified, so our personal relationship had strengthened and for the past three years we had spent virtually every working hour together. Our mutual interests and ambitions had become a love affair and it was almost inevitable that we would formalize that relationship. In November

1960 we dashed up to London and got married in Caxton Hall, by then a fashionable registry office, with just my sister, Betty, as a witness. Our wedding was followed by a quick Italian lunch in Soho Square (the heart of filmland – where else?) and then back to the Slough studios to finish shooting the titles for *Supercar*. We had no honeymoon or wedding reception, as there was just no time for any of this. It was not exactly a typical film wedding and I suppose I should have realized then where our real priorities lay.

No sooner had we wrapped production on *Supercar* than we received a call from Lew Grade, who fired questions at us about our next idea. This time we were ready for him. He gave us his full approval of *Fireball XL5*, which, as a reflection of the Space Age now upon us, was highly topical and marketable. Steve Zodiac was the typical astronaut hero, Venus, the blonde international New Woman. Relieved to be playing female parts again, I gave her a seductive continental voice. Professor Matic, Robbie and our space-pet animal, Zoony, completed our cast list. The sixties had now arrived and our characters and stories reflected the mood of the era: space exploration had begun in earnest and anything was possible.

I had fun with the creation of the characters and Gerry and I once more collaborated on the script. Our combined talents were complementary: his technical invention, with my artistic input and skills with characterization. This happy teamwork would continue for a number of years with outstanding success.

By 1962 Gerry and I were paying regular visits to the States as ATV's ambassadors. We visited American television stations and spoke a lot of high-powered jargon to smooth, well-heeled television executives in New York. Lew had sold our programme to American television at a time when very few British programmes made it there. We discussed future ideas with whoever happened to be sitting in the boss's chair at the time, in the hope of capturing their interest and paving the way for Lew's super salesmanship. The trouble was then, as now, that the rapid turnover of people at the top in the world of television often meant that by the time the show was completed, someone else would be in charge. They would slip into meetings unannounced and sit in silent observation, waiting to inherit the chair, but not necessarily the previous incumbent's ideas and projects.

I remember joking at the time that we always knew the measure of the success of our current show by the size of the limousine that met us at the airport. On just such a visit to the United States we saw colour television for the first time and on our return to Britain reported to Lew Grade our enthusiasm for this technological breakthrough. As we worked at least a year ahead of a programme's transmission, it was felt that our next production should be made in colour. Although this was untried and more costly than black-and-white transmission, we felt it was necessary for the sake of future sales: there was no way that a black-and-white production could compete with a colour version. Lew, as always aware of the market potential, quickly agreed, and so the very first colour television production went into development in the United Kingdom with *Stingray*. Of course there were teething problems we had not envisaged with this, but having overcome them we became pioneers in the field of colour television.

Stingray was a clear departure from the space exploits of *Fireball XL5* and explored the relatively peaceful underwater world. With the Marineville headquarters we had fun with some of the names, like Commander Shore and Troy Tempest. I had decided to give my voice a rest and concentrate on the scripts and characters, so I wrote in a silent heroine called Marina, who proved very popular with the male audiences. There were many proposals of marriage for the lovely, ethereal Marina, who never, but never, interrupted her male counterparts. Lois Maxwell – James Bond's Miss Moneypenny – played Commander Shore's assistant and Ray Barrett, an Australian actor – later famous for *The Power Game* – played the voice of Commander Shore. We would record on Sundays to allow the actors to fulfil their other acting commitments.

I have fond memories of those sessions where I had to behave somewhat like a kindergarten teacher, allowing the actors to catch up on their week's activities and pour out their personal stories before starting rehearsal. We often recorded three or four scripts in a day with an impossible number of different voices. These sessions were not without their dramas, such as when a young, bohemian Australian actor called Barry Humphries – fresh from the outback and not yet in drag – would regularly forget to turn up. When he did, though, he was quite brilliant, with a strong talent for female voices. In retrospect, this was a hint of things to come with his highly successful Dame Edna portrayal.

Now that we knew the working of Lew Grade's active mind, we

were already developing our next idea before the completion of *Stingray* in 1964. We had achieved the move to colour smoothly and ahead of our time and now we wanted to make another transition – to produce our first hour programme. To date the longest programmes had been a half-hour, which was quite normal for a children's show, but audience ratings and international sales now proved that our appeal was worldwide and embraced the whole family. Our market had grown and a 'kidult' show, as the Americans so aptly described our programmes, was the next step.

This was a difficult progression, both from the point of view of cost and programming. Personally, I was determined to push for the hour show, because as a writer it gave me extra scope to develop the characters, and inject them with more humour and personality, which, in turn, would upgrade the content of our shows and undoubtedly please our fans. Our merchandising operation, too, stood a better chance of marketing characters who were more finely developed. The hardware and cast of players could be more expensive and lend themselves more readily to by-products. Lew Grade, after some persuasion, but with typical bravura, took the financial gamble and the idea for *Thunderbirds* was born in 1963.

From the start, I knew that *Thunderbirds* would be a winner. I had been enthusiastic about all our series to date, but never before like this. It was sheer luxury for me to have an hour show with which to juggle and my imagination just ran riot. How about a character who lived in a stately home, had a cockney sidekick and worked for a secret service? What about an island headquarters and a family of handsome adventurers, an oriental member of the team, and a villainous bald-headed masterspy? They soon translated into Lady Penelope, Parker, Jeff Tracy and the International Rescue team. Derek Meddings came up with the ideas for the wonderful craft, and Gerry and I paid one of our many happy visits to a then unknown village in Portugal called Albufeira to write the pilot script.

It had become increasingly difficult to write either at home or at work (places which frequently overlapped) and one day, when lunching with Peter Gormley, Cliff Richard's personal manager, we mentioned that we were looking for a quiet hideaway in order to write, preferably with sunshine. Peter suggested Portugal and mentioned that Cliff and the Shadows all had places down there, as well as Frank Ifield, whose villa was currently available and we could stay there if we wanted. So, off we set, flying into Faro airport with no accommodation address, but a firm promise that we would be met on arrival. Of course, no one was there to meet us, something had gone wrong. The mention of Cliff Richard's name, however, worked like magic and a taxi whisked us off to Albufeira, where our love affair with the then unspoilt southern coast of Portugal began. Without doubt, the creation of *Thunderbirds* owes much to Peter Gormley's inspired suggestion. We later owned a place there, which became our second home for many years, but, in the early sixties, the whole project gelled in the soothing and exotic atmosphere of sea and sunshine. Away from the trading estate and in Albufeira, our minds could naturally envisage a South Sea island – the new secret headquarters for our International Rescue team – and the characters came easily to life.

For the moment, it seemed that all our knowledge that had gone before was now incorporated into *Thunderbirds*. Before we had shot one single foot of film all the national popular press arrived to camp outside the studio door and from its inception *Thunderbirds* was a success with viewers and media alike. In total we made thirty-two episodes and two full-length cinematic feature films over the period of 1963–7. It was as if all our previous work had been one big rehearsal for this one new series. The swinging sixties embraced our International Rescue team and their exploits without reservation. We were in the right time and in the right place and in the right company: *Thunderbirds* were definitely go!

2

THE THUNDERBIRDS YEARS

It is only by looking back and having time to reflect that it becomes possible to analyse the reasons for the phenomenal success of *Thunderbirds* that has endured for over twenty-five years and – at the time of writing – looks set to have a whole new lease of life with the programmes once more being screened on television and released on video. Being so personally involved in the creation and production of *Thunderbirds,* it is too easy just to accept the success and enjoy the continued loyalty of the fans and it was not until I came to write this book that I started to put everything in context. I came to realize that the years *Thunderbirds* spanned, between 1963 and 1968, were five of the most exciting years of the sixties and five of the happiest years of my life too. From its original conception to the completion of the thirty-two episodes and two feature films, much happened both personally to those of us involved in *Thunderbirds,* and generally in the world around us.

I believe that *Thunderbirds* is more than just a success story relating to a pioneering concept, but rather, like the Beatles, it represents a landmark in the lives of many people who were growing up in that era. Some of its cultural impact has endured over the years and has been taken up by younger generations. The mid-sixties saw the height of activity in what was dubbed Swinging London – the most fertile ground for new ideas and ventures, where anything and everything was possible. Old class barriers were crumbling, and love, peace and the heady pursuit of happiness and freedom were paramount. Of course, it was not always as idyllic as it sounded, and drugs, sex and rock 'n' roll did not always add up to the peace and love of flower power. For many it was a harmless, youthful era of fun and rebellion, while for others it was the short path to self destruction.

But, along with the culture freedom of the Beatles and the Rolling Stones came the arrival of Mary Whitehouse to monitor television material that was fast shedding its shackles of censorship and 'good taste'. Needless to say, *Thunderbirds* never offended – except by the accusation of being too 'transatlantic' – and we took our responsibilities seriously as the makers of family shows. We reflected the space-age achievements that were happening thick and fast around us. The race for space was on between North America and the Soviet Union and we were all thrilled to see the first moonwalk with the United States' Major Ed White in *Gemini 4*. This fired our imaginations and justified our inclusion of the *Thunderbirds* spacecraft in the International Rescue team, which later would crystallize and develop into our series with human actors, *UFO* made in 1969 and *Space 1999* five years later. The planet Mars was also being observed in space and space docking was pioneered. All in all such events constituted a science-fiction writer's dream.

Hollywood struggled to compete with the new space-age heroes and the outrageous rock stars. Ageing movie stars smoked pot, wore beads and languished in kaftans, some even joined the hippie communes in San Francisco. The beginnings of the feminist movement were budding and bras would soon be burned, but Lady Penelope did not burn her bras and the International Rescue team retained its clean-cut, space-hero image. The nearest we came to the popular culture was when Cliff Richard and the Shadows featured in the movie, *Thunderbirds Are Go!* This was an acceptable image for our impressionable audiences.

Mary Quant dominated the British fashion scene and influenced my designs for the series. Miniskirts had become the uniform, and I recall wearing my very first mini, rather self-consciously, to a Royal Variety Command Performance in the mid-sixties. Topping the bill was Tom Jones, in fine voice, and a group of young lads from Liverpool who were the latest rage. As we made our way through the crowd of screaming girls outside the London Palladium I assumed they were for Tom, until I saw a banner declaring, WE LOVE THE BEATLES. Their act did not really suit the venue and I remained unimpressed, as did the audience of showbusiness professionals around me. If I had been asked to sign them up then and there, I would not have bothered. For my taste, the Stones were much more exciting, but only time would tell me how wrong I was about the Beatles. Soon we were all caught up in Beatlemania and I was twisting the night away to 'Can't Buy Me Love' along with everyone else.

The first Bond movie came out then in 1962, with Sean Connery and Ursula Andress, and *Dr No*, still remains an early favourite of mine. We were intrigued. It had all the hallmarks of success and it was as if all our Supermarionation adventures had come to life. Sean Connery could easily have been one of my own creations: tall, dark and madly handsome – a real action man. Later, in 1969, we were approached by Harry Saltzman, one of the Bond producers, to make a Bond movie, but we were too involved in the production of *UFO* at the time and there were contractual problems that just could not be overcome.

While the concept of *Thunderbirds* was in its embryo stage, Gerry and I took time out to celebrate our third wedding anniversary. The date was 22 November 1963, memorable also for quite a different reason. As we rode in the taxi to our favourite restaurant for dinner, we saw special editions of newspapers being sold on the street, the headlines screaming the news of President Kennedy's assassination in Dallas, Texas. Everyone was in shock and the whole of London abuzz with stunned disbelief. We cancelled our anniversary celebration and headed for home, our festive evening suddenly turned into a sombre wake. Somehow our wedding anniversaries were never to be the same after this and later I thought that it may have been a bad omen.

There were many more events to touch our lives during the *Thunderbirds* years. The Conservative government was brought down by the Profumo Affair and Christine Keeler and Mandy Rice-Davies became the most photographed 'party girls' of their day, in the late 1980s also to become the subject of Michael Caton-Jones's film, *Scandal*. Twiggy forced us all to diet like mad and Vidal Sassoon cut our hair in his angular style so that we all emerged looking identically cropped.

Carnaby Street, the King's Road and Biba became my hunting ground for fashion ideas for my own wardrobe as well as those of the puppets, invariably with the strains of the latest Beatles smash-hit on the Muzak system in the background. In 1966 the Fab Four had been received at Buckingham Palace to collect their MBEs, which they accepted with disdain. They had become a law unto themselves by now and I wondered what had happened to those clean-cut young boys of the early days? Nevertheless, regardless of their private lives, their music continued to get better and better.

It was the following year, 1967, that ATV received the Queen's Award for Industry for exports and I would like to think that *Thunderbirds* contributed somewhat to that achievement by the sale of the programme overseas. Last, and by no means least, later that same year saw the arrival of our son Gerry Jun., now known in the family as Andy. Gerry Sen. was ecstatic and sent out cards announcing that 'Gerry and Sylvia Anderson are pleased to announce the birth of their son – their latest production.'

Lew Grade shared our news when we first learned that I was pregnant and he and Kathy, his wife, were most supportive during a difficult pregnancy when I had to spend a great deal of time supposedly resting, but fortunately able to work from home. Two days after the caesarian section, I was sitting up rather painfully in bed approving designs for *Joe 90*, our newest on-screen creation. The maternity unit, I am sure, was relieved to see me go home, glad to escape, as the day of filming approached, the inevitable stream of visits from our puppet team, armed with drawings, sketches and queries. Gerry's cute birth-announcement cards – a design complete with clapper-board and a roll of film – provoked a deluge of flowers which had to be diverted to the local general hospital. All I wanted to do was to have some quiet time with my new baby but, as always, the production line was rolling and demanded my attention.

A short while before, another Lady Penelope birth had taken place. Our beautiful Great Dane, named after our heroine, had given birth to nine gorgeous puppies without fuss or medical aid, so our household was brimming over with new arrivals. Penny, as she became known in the family, guarded Gerry Jun. with the same ferocity that she protected her own offspring. She remained with me until she was a graceful old lady of thirteen and died with the same dignity as she gave birth and she takes a special pride of place in my happy memories of that time, as do Bill and Sheila Harding, the married couple who took care of the domestic side of our life.

As the *Thunderbirds* series was coming to a close and we moved on to other projects, the sixties sound was beginning to hit a sour note. The Beatles lost their manager and mentor, Brian Epstein, who had committed suicide while his protégés meditated in India, trying to cope with their new-found success and the Stones, too, were in trouble – with the law – on a drugs' charge. Was the pop bubble about to burst, we asked ourselves? We hoped not. In the United States, Elvis Presley had not yet succumbed to chemical dependency and had just married his lovely schoolgirl bride, Priscilla. We all believed that they would live happily ever after. Well, it was the sixties after all and we were so naïvely full of hope.

By the end of 1967, we had completed filming thirty-two one-hour episodes and two feature films (*Thunderbirds Are Go!* and *Thunderbird Six*) and we already had *Captain Scarlet* in the can and *Joe 90* in pre-production. Thus *Thunderbirds* had already become old news, an earlier work, even though interest was still gathering momentum with the books and magazines featuring our International Rescue team. I was sad then to say goodbye to the characters who were no longer part of our shooting schedule, little knowing that it was really only the beginning of *Thunderbirds*.

3

CREATING THE CHARACTERS

Over the years I have often been asked how we came up with the ideas for our series and how Gerry and I worked together on them. In the beginning, it was very much a case of me being the new girl and taking the lead from Gerry and the other men around me. But with each series and the hands-on experience of our specialized form of film-making, I gained a new confidence. I was the main feminine influence in a male-dominated working world and from my role as Girl Friday with Polytechnic, I had become an executive and the co-creator of our Supermarionation series. I was also playing many voices and directing the actors who provided the dialogue. So, in the space of six short years from 1957 to 1963, I had come a long way. It had all been an amazing training in the basics of film-making and it was very rewarding to be able to develop my ideas through to fruition. Although I was part of a successful husband-and-wife business and creative partnership, I was also establishing myself in my own right, when it was quite rare for a women to be an executive with such a high profile. The press loved this. My success was novel to them and the popularity of my creation, Lady Penelope, combined to give them the perfect newsworthy angle that they always sought.

All the heroines in our previous series had been perfect foils to the action-man heroes, but now, with Lady Penelope, we had an action girl who was a personality in her own right. In a way, life was imitating art, as I began to find my own identity within the framework of our working life. However, I did not realize at the time that his would be the cause of much resentment in years to come. While I was perceived as merely the female contributor in the team and my female heroines walked several paces behind their action men, my role was acceptable to Gerry and, indeed, he encouraged and supported it. Once that position changed, however, so did the fine balance of our relationship. It is important to understand that I was not a crusading women's liberationist or anything like that, but I was growing and learning and starting to have a voice which did not always echo everything that Gerry pronounced. More importantly, I was beginning to have a public face with the growing popularity of the series and my *alter ego* Lady Penelope. Yet, during the scripting of the first episode and the development of the series, nothing was further from my mind.

In 1964 the problems had not yet surfaced and Gerry and I collaborated happily on *Thunderbirds,* as we had on other series in the past. As I have said already it was our first one-hour project and gave us an opportunity to develop our stories and characters to the full. I must admit that in retrospect it seems quite remarkable to me that we were able to come up with original and exciting ideas so regularly and so successfully. But in the environment in which we lived and worked, it was the most natural thing in the world. We had known so much hardship and disappointment in the early days, that having the luxury of ATV in our corner was sheer joy. We would go to Lew Grade with just the germ of an idea, often filling less than a page, and after talking it through with him we would leave his office with his full approval to proceed – all arranged in one meeting. This simply could not and does not happen in the nineties. Amazingly, good films *do* get made and young people do get the breaks, but now it is in spite of the system and not because of it.

Today there are too few Lew Grades in the film and television business who are willing to give a helping hand to the young hopefuls that we were when we first met him. Given that we were imaginative, enthusiastic and original in our ideas, we were also very fortunate too. That fact has often been overlooked in the retelling of the *Thunderbirds* success story. We were all part of a team that made up a unique and workable template. If the right pieces had not come together at the right time, then we would have just been another struggling small production company. I am pleased to have contributed to our good fortune by persisting when we were about to go out of business in the early days after *Four Feather Falls* and our rejection by Granada. At that time, Gerry recognized and admired what he called my Churchillian quality.

Previous page: Lady Penelope at home.

Left and below: Completing the wiring for a dramatic explosion at sea.

Right: Paddy Seale, making a final lighting check on the set.

FAB 1 Lady Penelope's ROLLS-ROYCE
as seen in 'THUNDERBIRDS'.
Hydraulic platform with fold down safety rails.
Swivel laser beam and smoke making apparatus. Set in rear wings.
Gull wing canopy and down-and-under doors.
Laminated, Anti-glare, bullet-proof glass-steel canopy.
Part of the top secret enormously powerful engine
Retro pack air brakes (fitted to both wings — indicated on off-side wing only.)
Rear Hydrofoil.
The hub cap motif extends on rod to form a tyre slasher. (On all wheels — foremost shown in normal position.)
FAB 1
Retractable studs for snow and ice. (Shown on one wheel only—fitted to all six).
Centre pull down armrests of back seat have retractable handcuffs and chest band.
Hydrofoils when fully lowered extend below level of wheels thus lifting whole car clear of water when at speed—minimizes resistance. The rear 'foil has a vortex-aquajet powerpack fitted centrally.

LONDON AGENT
LADY
PENELOPE

PILOT
THUNDERBIRD 1
SCOTT TRACY

PILOT
THUNDERBIRD 2
VIRGIL TRACY

ASTRONAUT
THUNDERBIRD 3
ALAN TRACY

Previous pages: The International Rescue Team celebrating Christmas. *From left to right*: Scott, Parker, Lady P, TinTin, Alan, Gordon, Virgil, Jeff and John.

These pages: Members of IRT with their craft, from the opening credits of *Thunderbirds Are Go!*, with The Hood *(below right)*.

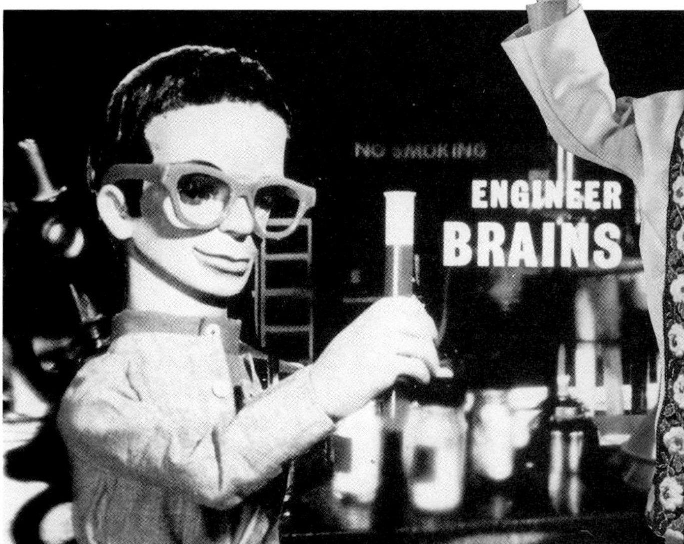

Right: Parker in a tight fix!

Below: Rescue vehicle, Thunderbird 2, leaves the island hangar on a mission.

But it is no one person's actions, rather a chain of events in life, that forms the whole pattern. Maybe, though, I triggered off that chain reaction to our advantage by refusing to give up.

We were in Portugal putting our ideas on paper and devising the pattern for the *Thunderbirds* series, which had been going round our heads for several months. Now was the time to mix the vital ingredients, to establish the characters and background for International Rescue out of which the series narrative would evolve. Back in the studio the team anxiously awaited our production of the bible, as it is called: the document that creates the blueprint for the whole series concept.

Gerry and I worked well together: we respected our individual ideas and talents, which rarely overlapped. Generally speaking, there was a division of labour, whereby I would create the characters and Gerry would devise the action sequences of the plot. The storyline was a blend of the two. On completion of the script, we would pursue our respective areas of production: I followed through with the development of the characters – designing the clothes and casting the voices; Gerry would liaise with Reg Hill and Derek Meddings over the effects and the hardware content, such as the vehicles and the craft. John Read was versatile enough to become involved in all the various aspects of the production, as both a practical artist and cameraman. Slowly, bit by bit, the pieces were forged together and the final picture emerged.

During the sixties, a social revolution was taking place and young debutantes no longer dressed in twin sets and pearls or paired with men who were chinless wonders. Now there were the likes of Georgie Fame and Alan Price of the Animals, hulled from working-class districts of the north-east of England; Mick Jagger living with Marianne Faithfull, who was the daughter of a baroness; Paul McCartney and his posh girlfriend, Jane Asher. There were young actors around town just making it in the movie world, like Michael Caine and Terence Stamp, who fascinated the Home Counties girls like designer Edina Ronay and model Jean Shrimpton. It was difficult now to distinguish between a working girl and the finishing-school product; each would be wearing the sixties uniform of minis and trendy hair cut, and be on the pill.

Lady Penelope was the last of a dying breed of debutantes, but even she was breaking ranks as the London agent of International Rescue. I wrote her in with not only the daring and panache of a secret agent, but also the poise of a cool and beautiful aristocrat. She was not the obvious choice for an action girl, but one that to me had exciting possibilities. I also had to consider the American market and knew that they would love a typical British lady. Once I had outlined her picture in my mind I decided that she had to have a British partner. After all, she could not sit alone in that vast mansion and only talk by remote to Jeff and the boys. So, what better than a faithful old retainer in which to confide and share her adventures? 'Nosey' Parker, as he had been known in his younger days, thus became the comic element of the duo.

In order to write the characters I had to invent and visualize their back story, that is to say their background, everything that happened to the character prior to their appearance on screen: their childhood, their social and emotional profile, their biography. Lady P was easy – a top drawer, impeccable pedigree – and so Parker had to be invented in sharp contrast. He emerged as a lovable rogue with doubtful connections, who had now gone straight. I soon conceived a link between them in the back story when Lady P visits Parker in prison during one of her benefactory forays into the world, doing charitable acts. She helps him on his release from prison by offering him the job of manservant and chauffeur, making him the perfect partner – if not in crime – at least in adventure. There probably is no such thing now as a lovable rogue, but in the sixties it was still a whimsical notion.

Having established Lady Penelope and Parker in the cast of characters, the rest of the team evolved: Jeff Tracy, as the head of International Rescue, was an ex-astronaut, much in keeping with the flavour of the space age in which we were living, and he worked well. I continued brainstorming and felt inspired by other current television programmes of the time, such as *Bonanza*, which was highly successful in the mid-sixties. Here I got the idea of having more than one hero. How about several brothers and sons of Jeff Tracy, each with a distinct look, a distinct personality? There would still be the father figure of Jeff, who was attractive and adventurous, yet an interesting counterpart for Lady P. With more than one hero, there was also an opportunity to widen our audience appeal. As it turned out, each son acquired a devoted following, but the most popular were the blond, baby-faced Alan and the darkly handsome Scott.

Our cast of regular players was beginning to come together but no drama would be complete without the arch villain. Thus the Hood was created and became the character that everyone loved to hate. A master of disguise, with an almost psychopathic hatred of International Rescue, he featured heavily in the opening episodes, but never really seized the imagination of the audience – at least not nearly as much as we had hoped. But his role as antagonist was a vital one: he was the necessary evil.

Among the male-dominated team, we had to redress the balance by creating the beautiful TinTin, Jeff Tracy's assistant. I created a back story for her in the first episode that somehow got forgotten along the way. When I wrote her in, she was the daughter of Jeff Tracy's faithful manservant, Kyrano, and arrives on the island after being involved in a near fatal plane disaster from which she is saved by International Rescue. Kyrano is subconsciously under the spell of his half-brother, the evil Hood and reveals the secret existence of the newly formed International Rescue. Kyrano was a character who was difficult to develop and gradually he became reduced to cameo appearances, like the Hood. Although TinTin had her followers, she was mostly island bound and did not get the same opportunities as Lady P for outside adventures. She was, nevertheless, a decorative sidekick to her macho boss.

Brains was yet another version of our regular boffin-type characters who had appeared in all our previous series: as Dr Beaker in *Supercar;* Professor Mathew Matic in *Fireball XL5* and Phones in *Stingray*. This professional whiz-kid was a very popular character and remains so today. We did, however, have problems with the American market over Brain's speech delivery. The voice (as played by David Graham, who was also, incidentally, the voice of Parker) had been evolved in the recording studio and as we all considered it an original interpretation, I gave it the go ahead. Brains had the hesitant speech of a young man preoccupied and confident with his work and experiments, yet socially unsure of himself. Unfortunately, it was one of those experiments that worked better in the recording studio than on the screen, and recently when I recorded a radio commercial with Brains, we experienced the same difficulty with getting the message across in a ten-second slot. The problem, on screen, was that Brains's hesitant delivery held up the action, which the Americans always demanded should move along fast, bearing in mind that the puppet action was slow enough without any speech impediments. The problem was overcome by giving Brains short lines and brief appearances, sometimes without dialogue. He has nevertheless endured as one of the *Thunderbirds* favourites.

One of the essential requirements of the *Thunderbirds* production schedule created a huge problem: it was necessary to have a backlog of scripts written ahead of filming, in order to have the puppets and sets built in time for production. This meant that the script went ahead with new developments of character and narrative, before their feasibility had been tried and proven on the screen. Given these parameters of practicality, some characters in the series inevitably worked better than others and account for there being, in later episodes, less of the Hood and less of Kyrano, both of whom turned out to be less viable on the screen than on the page.

However long the pre-production period is, it is never long enough. Like a writer's deadline, which looms ominously on the horizon, usually ending in a mad panic to meet the date, our deadlines were always tough and allowed little room for error. Everything had to be created from scratch in our miniature world and for the most part there was no outside supplier of standard items and props, as one would normally expect in film production. This put a great deal of pressure on us all and not least on our overworked puppet workshop and art department. With the design of new craft, Derek Meddings was always in a race against time.

By now, in 1963, we had leased a studio complex in a newly built factory, and installed it ourselves to our demanding design specifications. The empty shell was quickly transformed into a new, streamlined and compact studio complex for our ever growing departments. Such was our relationship with ATV that when we had asked for new premises, they had agreed readily. It was still on the same trading estate in Slough and just a stone's throw away from our last studio, which we had rapidly outgrown. I can remember driving to work each day past row upon row of dreary factory buildings and wondering whatever had happened to my dreams of Hollywood! Slough was a far cry from the dreams of Tinseltown on which I had been weaned. Once inside our studio door, however, I forgot my disappointment and became absorbed in our magical, miniature world.

As our action became more ambitious, so the demands on the visual-effects team grew. In turn, they required extra scope, which meant employing more people and having to find room to accommodate them. Now we had almost our entire operation under one roof:

merchandising, accounts and the production offices; the puppet workshops, art department and cutting-rooms; wardrobe, the shooting stages, and viewing theatre; a full-time workshop for building our sets and hardware; and, of course, a canteen. We constructed a mini film studio, unique by virtue of our creation of Supermarionation and the only one of its kind in the country. Everyone fought hard for their particular department, but, inevitably, there were disappointments. My wardrobe department, for example, even in the new studios, was still inadequately housed. Our wardrobe mistress, Betty Coleman, gave me a hard time because of my lack of success with my boys' own group. But, in time, having lost a few battles along the way, we won our war, but not before Betty had departed in protest and her place had been taken by the delightful Iris Richens. Iris was our cheerful canteen lady, who had sometimes helped out with the puppet wardrobe and I quickly spotted that her talents were of much more value in the manufacture of the small costumes. My faith in her was totally justified and she went on to become an expert wardrobe mistress, both on our own and on other productions. This was one of the advantages of running your own operation: it was possible to give opportunities to people who showed promise, but did not necessarily have the relevant experience. I also applied this principle to untried actors, who were just waiting to be given a chance to shine. To me, this is one of the most exciting aspects of the film business and it is rare to have the luxury to do this in the financially restrictive and corporate film-production climate of the 1990s.

4

THE CHARACTERS IN ACTION

Ever since the days of *Supercar*, we had continually to refine and devise methods of production to suit our special needs. We shot on film, as opposed to tape, in order to maintain the high broadcast quality that was necessary for good definition when transmitted on other television broadcast systems. *Thunderbirds* sold to over ninety-eight territories throughout the world, after all.

Over time, it became necessary to deal with the physical limitations of filming sets and characters a third of life-size. Camera angles were almost floor level, because of the scale, and we had installed television monitors on a closed circuit so as to give both the puppeteers and the crew a clear view. The director was housed in a glass booth, where he could observe the action on his own monitor and give his instructions on talkback. This method was quite commonplace in a television tape studio, but at that time was not used on film. Also housed in the booth was the lip-synch operator who keyed in the puppets during dialogue sequences. We had refined the puppet brain so that a small solenoid cell in the head overcame the problem of the conventional string in the manual operation of the puppet mouth movement. The puppeteer had always reacted to the taped voice with a split-second delay, which, with our invention, was eliminated. The dialogue was pre-recorded and the solenoid cells reacted to the voice on the tape. It was a pretty foolproof system and served us well throughout our puppet career.

But not everything on the puppet floor went quite as smoothly. The puppet operators on their seven-foot gantry often suffered from the heat of the arc lights. These were necessary for filming, but sometimes reached over 120°F. There was also a limit to the durability of the puppets themselves. For a variety of reasons, a scene would often have to be repeated over and over again, resulting in some bizarre misbehaviour by the puppet characters. Their operating wires had been specially developed so that they were strong enough to take the weight required, but virtually invisible to the camera eye. Despite our care, however, a wire would snap inexplicably at times rendering the puppet impotent. Then, too, with complicated action, wires would tangle and brain seizures were commonplace. Such were the joys of Supermarionation, which made dealing with actors at a later date comparatively uncomplicated.

But prior to the shooting stage, there was the tortuous route of pre-production. Once the script was passed as workable, we would start the first of many production meetings, involving the respective heads of production departments. In spite of intimate knowledge of the limitations of Supermarionation, invariably we would ask the impossible of our working team, whether it be an over complicated special-effects shot or an ambitious puppet action. But our talented team rarely let us down and it was a challenge that they rose to with great determination, although not without some misgivings. Would we ever be satisfied? they must have often wondered, always to receive the answer, no. We never were! Each series – each episode – had to be better than the last.

Inevitably my memory of this time is from my own perspective and with this in mind, I set out to track down some of the members of the crew, in order to gather their recollections of those hectic *Thunderbirds* years. Their recall was surprisingly sharp and detailed and I gleaned innumerable behind-the-scenes stories.

I met up with John Read again after a gap of many years. One of the original team of five, we had first met back in the late fifties when we had all worked together at Polytechnic.

When AP Films had started in 1957, John was the last to join the breakaway group, and on doing so, no one could have worked harder to make a success of the new venture. He and Reg Hill had worked together originally for National Interest Pictures as animation/title artists, John also doubling in rostrum camerawork. He tells of the time when Roger

Moore, a junior trainee, forgot to collect some important footage for processing at Kays laboratory. As a result, his training with the company was swiftly terminated. This turned out to be the best thing that had ever happened to him. When John next saw him, he was walking down Wardour Street in full film make-up and hailed John cheerfully with an actor's trained voice, well on his way to becoming a star. By the time they met up again at the Television Society Awards ceremony in the early sixties, he was filming the successful television series, *The Saint.*

John contributed greatly to our success – or, should I say, survival – in the early days when all our profits were ploughed back into AP Films. He even cashed in his £200 life-insurance policy to contribute to the ailing finances of the company. Between productions, he would do nightwork as a rostrum camera-operator, and he joined forces with us on the post-synching of Frankie Howerd in the film comedy, *Further Up the Creek.*

There is a definite art to post-synching, a technique which involves matching mouth movement to reworded dialogue. In the late fifties, when sound equipment was not as sophisticated as it is today, there would often be poor sound quality on locations, which meant that a sound-track would require re-recording in a sound-proofed studio. Now Frankie Howerd is a brilliant artist, but quite hopeless at revoicing his own dialogue, because, as an instinctive performer, he rarely repeats a line or an intonation in exactly the same way. His mouth movement, therefore, often failed to match the newly recorded dialogue. As most of the film had been re-recorded, we spent hours on it; it was a nightmare crash course in film editing techniques for me and one I shall never forget. Gerry was the trained editor; John and I the assistants, and ever since then I have held the greatest respect for the much neglected cutting-room team. It is where the final version of a film can stand or fall.

John was always a willing and practical, hands-on contributor at the studio. When it became vital to sound-proof our first studio, situated on a busy main road, he visited a local egg-packing station and came back with the company van full of 1500 egg cartons. These we stuck to the walls and roof and thus provided an instantly effective, and cheap, solution to the noise problem.

John also worked patiently with Reg Hill to perfect and pioneer an electronic lip-synch device, which was later developed by a company in Birmingham. The device was first used on *Four Feather Falls*, our puppet western. It was not without its teething problems: the puppet mouth would often open and stay open, or refuse to react to certain vowel sounds. With each new series, however, the system became more refined and by the time we came to shoot *Thunderbirds* most of these problems had been overcome. In these early days, Gerry and I both worked the rather primitive switchboard that keyed in the puppet mouths, a forerunner to our unique system that was used to perfection in *Thunderbirds*.

Another experiment, on *Four Feather Falls*, was made with the viewfinder of the camera. Because of the difficulties with the miniature – one third life-size – puppets and sets, a television camera augmented the use of the eyepiece. This enabled the director and camera operator to have a clear view of the scene. It was gradually improved by adapting an Arriflex viewfinder system and John worked closely with a local optical company to do this. An outside company later adapted it and with further refinements, it became commonly used in the industry. We were constantly breaking new ground with our miniature film world.

John Read wrote a piece on our puppet technology for *New Scientist* in December 1965. It was during our Supermarionation days and clearly describes our technique at that time and the problems we had to overcome:

> Essentially, what we are doing is simply film making: but film making in full colour, with the complications of having actors that are puppets one-third life-size. Because of this the script cannot be as straightforward as one written for a normal production.
>
> We must continually write around the puppet's limitations so that they appear, for example, to walk through doors (although the control wires make this impossible) or pick up a coffee cup (although their fingers are not in fact jointed).
>
> Our actors cannot talk, so we must record the dialogue before we start to shoot the film. The sound-track is played back as the film is being shot and in order to synchronise the movement of the mouth with the words, we had to devise a method of electrically connecting the puppets' heads with the tape-deck amplifier and also, of course, a means of ensuring that the right puppet 'speaks'.
>
> *Thunderbirds* and its predecessors make considerable use of special effects: up to 50 per cent of the film may be thus classed. We shoot the special effects and the activities of the puppets separately,

on different sets, to avoid problems of scale. An airliner exploding in flight, for example, may be no more than six inches long or so.

Special effects are, of course, the star attraction and since everything is shot in the studio, there is a big and unceasing programme of model and landscape-building. Even a storm at sea must be shot on the stage in a tank – an overflowing one to prevent a false 'horizon' – with fans creating a force 9 gale and arc-welding equipment providing the lightning. Explosions provide much of the excitement – during shooting as well as in the finished film. The special-effects department is continually devising new kinds of explosions and has quite different recipes for an oil rig blowing up and for the detonation of a nuclear power plant. For fire shots, a man operates a smoke generator – a blowlamp affair that burns refined diesel oil to produce non-hazardous fumes . . . When the palm trees sway, it's a fan operated to create the breeze . . .

Special effects scenes are filmed at up to 120 frames a second, compared with the 24 frames a second of normal cinematography, which has the effect of greatly slowing down motions, so that, for example, the explosion of an egg-cup full of gunpowder lasts as long as the explosion of a 1000-lb. bomb, and thus appears to have the same magnitude . . . Sound is constantly a problem in all these special effects. What, for example, is the sound made by a nuclear-powered vehicle whilst travelling through space? None at all, perhaps: but while silence used sparingly can heighten the drama, noise of some kind usually improves the atmosphere of this kind of film. So the effects department is kept busy recording sounds appropriate to machines and vehicles that so far exist only in the hands of the model maker.

An early optical problem with the photography was parallax, arising out of the close-range photography the work needed. A director of live actors can stand beside the camera and obtain virtually the same view as the cameraman. When the actors are but a foot or two from the camera, anyone alongside gets a view of the scene quite different from that of the cameraman himself. So director, art director, set dresser, and so on, had to queue for a look through the camera lens – a time-consuming business.

Even worse off were the puppeteers, who operated from a bridge seven feet above the set. For one thing, they could not see the puppets' eyes, so the camera crew had to shout directions until puppets who were conversing were looking in the appropriate direction. The answer, as we found, to both difficulties is a small television camera, looking into the camera's eyepiece, with monitors set in suitable positions.

This idea has since been adopted commercially, and equipment with these electronic viewfinders should soon be available. The next step for us will be to record on to videotape, which we shall be able to play back immediately to check for faults.

There are still many things we would like the puppets to do – have more mobile features, for example, and more live hands. While wires remain our main communication we are very restricted but have hopes soon of introducing radio control, to broadcast instructions via a receiver in each puppet's head. The scope for technical development is immense, in a field that fascinates us at the studio no less than it satisfies our audience.

John and I talked a lot about the very early days of the late fifties. Our first film, we remembered, was *Crossroads to Crime* which was as bad as it sounds. It starred Miriam Karlin, Anthony Oliver and Ferdy Mayne and it hardly ranks as one of our best efforts. But, it was work and we had our names on screen. It had all started one day in 1960 when Gerry informed us that important visitors would be looking around the studio. They came from a company called Anglo Amalgamated, which our switchboard operator always amused us by calling Anglo Mealgamated. They made typical British B-movies on modest budgets – and it showed. The partners were Nat Cohen and Stuart Levy, both very well known in Wardour Street at the time. Stuart Levy was recently widowed and, I would guess, in late middle age. Anyway, I duly showed them around and they seemed impressed, but I do not remember either having a great deal to say, or obviously making a stunning impression.

The next day, however, Stuart Levy phoned Gerry and asked to see him urgently in his office. We were all thrilled, imagining that he wanted to discuss a film or work of some sort. We had already mentioned a project in the pipeline, but had not expected such a prompt response. It transpired, though, that Levy was attracted to me and wanted to meet me again. Could Gerry arrange it? I am ashamed to say that we took advantage of his interest in me to seal a deal on *Crossroads to Crime*.

Later, when Gerry and my wedding plans were discreetly revealed to him, things were never quite the same and we had a rough ride in our dealings with the company.

Other live-action production that involved us prior to our ATV days were three commercials for Blue Cars, a travel firm. They were put our way by Nicholas Parsons, the voice of Tex Tucker in *Four Feather Falls*. John remembered being on location in Switzerland to shoot the commercials, which starred Nicholas, when the unit ran out of money. There was no money even to buy a drink; they had totally overspent the budget. Despite such problems, however, we received top television awards, alongside Benny Hill and other television stars of the day. As unknowns, this inspired some envious comments, and we expected it to lead to offers of work. Nothing happened, as is so often the way with awards, which are great ego boosters, bur rarely lead to a rush of work. I have often heard it said by Oscar winners that however nice it is to be honoured by one's peers, it does not always pay the rent.

John has his own company now, called Cinemation, which, with puppeteer, Mary Turner, has produced several series, including over 100 episodes of *Rupert the Bear* and fifty-two ten-minute episodes of *Clopa Castle*. They have also just completed a pilot for their own new series, *Spaced-Out Pirates*. Theirs is an extremely clever and artistic partnership, in which they work continuously. Currently they are involved in Japanese automation projects in their workshop studios in Surrey.

Mary Turner was one of our key puppeteers from the days of *Torchy* in 1959 and remained with us until the closure of the puppet studios at Slough in 1969. A modest, but infinitely talented person, she worked with Christine Glanville, our chief puppeteer, as a punctilious colleague, and paid meticulous attention to detail. During pre-production, she made many of the leading puppet characters and, during shooting, operated from the puppeteers' bridge.

Over the years Mary sculpted several of the main characters: Grandpa Twink, Ma Jones, Rocky the Horse and Jake in *Four Feather Falls;* Mike Mercury and Mitch in *Supercar;* Troy Tempest and Marina in *Stingray;* Captain Scarlet himself; Joe 90's Father; and Lady Penelope, John and Gordon in *Thunderbirds*. A former art teacher, she often experimented with improvements on the puppet design and tried to make bendable rubber hands during the creation of *Four Feather Falls*. Unfortunately, they were not successful as there was an adverse reaction between the latex rubber and copper wires. In 1960, there was no other rubber available and other kinds of wire broke too easily. The idea was developed later by an outside firm, but by this time *Thunderbirds* was in production.

Mary also experimented with our first under-control puppets – that is puppets without over-head operation wires – for the *Thunderbirds* series. This was highly successful and further developed for our later series, although its use was limited and mainly employed in close-ups.

The procedure of making the puppet characters was a tedious and exacting one. First, there was the initial sculpting of the Plasticine head, roughly painted and wigged, then photographed from all angles once the face itself was approved. This was followed by the process of making the head permanent: first cast in rubber, from which a bondaglass shell would be moulded. Bondaglass, incidentally, revolutionized the making of the puppet heads. It was a specially developed, glass-fibre cloth with a polyester resin. The shell was sanded down carefully and the leather insert slotted in below the lips to allow the mouth movement. Sanding down the puppet was laborious and vital; it had to be immaculately smooth in order to proceed to the final stage of painting. For our bit-part players, incidentally, plastic shells were used as the base – an improvement on the Plasticine heads previously used for guest artists.

Before the puppet could be painted, the eyeballs were first spring-loaded into socket bearings and, coupled with a track rod, ready to be hand operated from above. These were specially manufactured plastic eyes, produced by an independent optical company to our specifications. The eye rod had to be connected to the control wire for the manipulators to achieve the eye movement and even then the eyes could only move from side to side on the limited track fitment. To increase the scope of the puppet's eye movement, a separate head was produced, with a different action, whereby the eyes could blink. There was no possibility, however, of having both side-to-side head movements and blinking in any one head. Such were the drawbacks of our miniature actors.

After fitting the eye and mouth movements, the electronic 'brain' was installed through a flap in the back of the skull and operated by the magnetism between a steel plate and a solenoid, which opened the mouth, to be closed by a spring. The dialogue was pre-recorded on tape and of the eleven tungsten wires (5 thou thick), which activated each puppet, two carried impulses from the playback circuit to a solenoid in the head. This activated the hinged lower lip, thus synchronizing the lip movements with the speech.

Having thus equipped the character with eyes, mouth and an electronic brain, the final wigging and painting could be completed. It was then – and only then – that the puppet maker could be sure that the original version had been achieved and that no quirk of human error had evolved. More photographs would then be taken and compared with the originals to ensure a consistent likeness.

On the *Thunderbirds* series, plastic bodies – of standard male and female prototype – were manufactured by outside contractors, together with feet and hands. The weight of each puppet was 7–9lb. The exact balance was essential: if the body was too light, it would not respond to control, and if too heavy, it would impose a strain on the hair-fine, steel control wires.

The more realistic our puppets became, the more problems we had with them performing the mundane human actions of walking, standing up and sitting down in shot; of picking up objects; of all the simple movements which the human body performs with such ease. It was just possible to get away with the awkward moments in *Thunderbirds* because the proportions of the characters were still in caricature. It was later when we had developed a more realistic approach – as with *Captain Scarlet* in 1967 – that the still imperfect walk was the more obvious. Even with Supermarionation, there was a limit to the realism of the puppet action.

Each permanent character had at least four different heads which had to be taken from the original rubber mould, in order to achieve the various expressions, once again impossible for our limited puppet actors on one head. There was therefore a frowning head, a smiling head and a blinking head, in addition to the 'normal' expression. As John Read mentions in *New Scientist*, the next stop was to be remote-control puppets, but that proved too costly and required too much experimentation, so busy were we churning out a new series each year. That really was too far in the future even for us. In any case we found by critical reaction that the audience was just not interested in the exact science of the perfect, humanized puppet. They preferred our *Thunderbirds* version.

Another important aspect of the puppet creations was how to dress them. Not only were the miniature clothes tedious to make, but they also had to allow freedom of movement for the puppeteers to be able comfortably to operate their puppets. There was often a conflict between design and the practical requirements of the operators. Looking back, it is clear that such difficulties arose in trying to cater to too many demands. There was no real training for this kind of costume designer, since our type of production was unique, and it all involved much trial and error, although most of the women puppeteers became accustomed to making their own costumes for their stage characters.

During the production of *Thunderbirds*, our wardrobe lady, Betty Coleman, was not an experienced puppeteer and it was sometimes difficult for her to appreciate the problems of dressing in relation to technical puppet movement. However, she and her department did a wonderful job and it was a mammoth task. During the filming of *Thunderbirds Are Go!*, we had over 700 miniature costumes in stock. For the film itself over 150 additional costumes had to be made, often in duplicate or triplicate, in case of damage or loss, without which the production would be delayed and cost dearly.

I usually designed the main characters' clothes, but left the guest wardrobe to the enterprising wardrobe department, always keeping an eye open for any outfits that did not gel with the rest of the designs. Of course, I went to town with Lady P's wardrobe and Lew Grade got carried away during an interview prior to the completion of the series, saying that we would have top Paris designers for her clothes. I should perhaps have adopted a trade name for the label!

When it came to making Lady Penelope, there was some difficulty in getting just the right face to match my mental picture of her. The script called for her to be cool, aristocratic and classy, but sexy too. Yet, she was not a caricature, like Parker, for example, and the look had to be just right for her as International Rescue's new London agent. Mary worked steadily and kept appearing with yet another remodelled plasticine head, but by the time the weekend arrived, we were no nearer achieving the correct image. I suggested that she should take a break and we would make a fresh start on Monday. On Monday, however, Mary appeared with a newly modelled face, which I liked immediately; it seemed vaguely familiar and I made a few minor comments, suggesting that she should remodel the mouth to make it more like Judith Shutt's, one of the other team members. Mary returned with the alterations and I was happy for our heroine to be 'cast'. It was thus that Lady P was born!

It was not until much later, when we were actually in production and Lady P was already a star, that I heard the true story about her creation. During a press interview, I was asked on whom Lady P had been based and replied that it was a matter of trial and error. For a blow-by-blow account of her creation, though, I suggested that they question Mary Turner, her ladyship's sculptor. It was then I learned, to my amazement, that Mary had modelled her on me. Her exact quote when describing her work, in a later interview with the *Daily Mirror* in 1968, maintained that:

> Sylvia discusses with me what type of characters and costumes she wants for the whole series. We model the characters roughly on real people – she might say, 'I want someone looking like Adam Faith,' for example – and I interpret her ideas. Lady Penelope, by the way, was modelled on Sylvia herself – we wanted a glamorous blonde and she was the obvious choice.

It was just as well I was unaware at the time that I was the role model, as I might have had an attack of false modesty and rejected Mary's version on principle. As it was, by the time I knew, she was already an established star. It was a bit like looking in the mirror and not recognizing your own reflection.

Mary's organizational skills and attention to detail ensured that our puppet content was always of the highest quality, and we owe her a great deal for her contribution during the Supermarionation years.

John Brown was one of our key puppet makers from the days of *Fireball XL5*. When I asked him recently why he had decided to join us in 1961, he gave me a crisp, pragmatic answer: we had offered him £3.00 a week more than he was earning already. It was not quite the answer I had expected. I had imagined he might say that it was his fascination for filming and the new, exciting medium we were creating, but John is a practical person and I am sure he was partially speaking the truth. I am also sure, though, that he was attracted by our enthusiasm and energy as John stayed with us for several years, right up to the making of *Captain Scarlet* in 1967. I watched him tackle every problem and demand of the increasingly ambitious puppetry, with a quiet Midlands humour and an enormous capacity for hard work. By the time it came to make *Thunderbirds Are Go!* in 1966, he was head of the puppet workshop.

Although there was nothing essentially glamorous, and everything highly practical, about the puppet workshop, it held an endless fascination for the steady stream of visitors, who were intrigued by the cast of characters on the assembly line, in various stages of creation and repair. But, mostly, for those who worked there it involved long hours of tedious graft: sculpting, remodelling and coping with the problems peculiar to puppets one-third of life-size. In the pre-production period the work of creating and building the main characters was carried out, but during the production itself, there were always running repairs and guest characters to produce. To me, the workshop resembled a giant dolls' hospital, with an array of limbs and spare parts on continual display.

I had always been fascinated by toy-repair shops as a child and remember visiting our local dolls' hospital on every possible pretext. All of this intrigued and scared me a little, too, but still remains a very clear memory where other, possibly more important events are blurred. The dim, dusty museums of half-repaired and sometimes forgotten dolls is probably my only vague, early connection with puppets. Over the years I have often been asked if I made puppets or had a puppet theatre as a girl, and my negative answer is always a surprise. Perhaps, though, my childhood memory served to nourish and develop a make-believe world, the inevitable forerunner to my world of the 'little people'.

I worked closely with John, as I did with all the other puppet makers, on the creation of the characters. In the scripts, having first created them I also had a strong mental picture which required additional translation into a 22-inch puppet being. This is where close communication with the puppet makers became essential. John had previously worked on *Stingray* and had worked on Jeff Tracy and Virgil, one of his sons. He also produced a host of guest characters, and kept up the unavoidable running repairs. Probably, though, John's greatest achievement at that time was the puppet version of Cliff Richard for our cinema feature *Thunderbirds Are Go!* For the first time he had a real-life model who would be compared and scrutinized in minute detail, and so accuracy was especially important and involved visits to Cliff and the Shadows in their recording studio, where facial proportions were measured and a series of reference photographs taken.

When I spoke to John again recently, he reminded me that I had rejected his first effort to re-create Cliff. This was much to his own great dismay as well as that of his departmental colleagues who for weeks had watched him work painstakingly on the face. I only remember that the final version, approved by me, was brilliant, and a great credit to John's talent and endless patience. It had been an especially demanding brief as, apart from the facial likeness of Cliff and the Shadows, their movements on stage had to be studied and copied for the film. I had written in a dream sequence in which Lady Penelope, with Parker, of course, goes into space with Alan and FAB 1 to visit a night club called the Swinging Star. When they arrive, the cabaret is provided by Cliff and the Shadows. Cliff and the boys wrote the musical sequence and pre-recorded a number sung by Cliff called 'Shooting Star'. The sequence was stunning and proved the highlight of the film.

Another of John's puppet creations was the Hood, our arch villain. John had the uncanny knack of translating my thoughts and ideas brilliantly into a puppet character. At my suggestion, he would change a nose, strengthen a chin, widen the eyes, until the written image became actual. We often used famous faces as role models, once experimenting with a composite face, using what we considered the best of each star: Elizabeth Taylor's eyes, Marilyn Monroe's mouth, Sophia Loren's nose. This was a dismal failure, proving that perfection only works in the right setting and the idea was quickly jettisoned.

John was eclectic in his gathering of ideas and I was intrigued to learn that he often studied faces at airports for inspiration. I had found myself doing just that too, so that every time I made a journey I would sit in the airport lounge and study the sea of faces. By doing this, I realized that there were, in fact, a limited number of basic face structures, the rest only variations on a theme, allowing for age, health and individual character. Heart-shaped, the classic oval, the square jaw, the round face, the long, thin shape and the angular: each individual face belonged to one of these categories. Often the same shape mouth or nose belonged to the same basic shape category and made the task of facial permutations that much easier.

John remembered a typical near disaster that seemed to dog every production: on the eve of shooting the *Thunderbirds* series, the wrong size hands had been delivered from the outside contractors and had to be replaced instantly as they would, of course, have looked ludicrous on the characters. In retelling the story, John hastened to reassure me that the fault did not lie with his own department. If it had, though, I would not have blamed them, as no group of people would have worked harder.

Each puppet maker had their own regular character to sculpt, according to their particular talents. Parker, the most highly caricatured member of the cast, was made by John Blundall, who had originally introduced John Brown to us. I felt it was a clever interpretation of my initial idea to base Parker on a fifties comedian – Ben Warris, of Jewel and Warris fame. Fortunately for us, he was to become even more famous than his human prototype.

Of all the puppeteers it was a local girl, a talented and pretty student called Wanda, who had the knack with Lady P's hair-dos – custom-made wigs of real hair. She and John Brown fell in love and married; they have already celebrated their Silver Wedding anniversary. John is currently working on the movie, *Aliens III* at Pinewood Studios. For him, as for so many people, our Supermarionation studio provided a crash course in a very specialized area of film production.

Some of the romances and marriages that began at the studios did not withstand the test of time and I can think of at least half a dozen such marriages that have since ended in divorce. During the *Thunderbirds* era, though, we were all still at the honeymoon stage. We were optimistic and committed to our work with all the enthusiasm of youthful discovery.

5

TECHNICAL WIZARDRY

If I were asked to single out one person from our Supermarionation team and evaluate their contribution to our success, it would have to be Derek Meddings, our visual effects director. He remained with us throughout our Supermarionation career, from our initial projects in 1957, through to our live-action productions, *Doppelgänger* and *UFO* in the late sixties and early seventies.

I first met Derek when he came to work for us when we were making *Twizzle*. At that time he was moonlighting, working by day as a matte artist at Shepperton Studios, and by night with us, painting scene backings. When I talked with him recently, I asked him how he had rated our chances then of making it big. His reply was that he had been unimpressed: in his eyes, although hard working and enthusiastic, we were still only producing a puppet show and not live action. The real thing, in Derek's book, was live action, accustomed as he was to working on productions such as the Hammer horror movies at Bray Studios.

Derek worked for a special effects company run by Les Bowie, a much respected film technician. AP Films had approached him with a view to working with us, a proposition which Les declined graciously as he was not really interested in our group. We must have appeared unlikely business partners, based in a ramshackle country house, filming puppets in front of a painted backdrop. In any case, he pointed Derek in our direction. Derek was married with a young family and needed the money, he was equally as unenthusiastic about us as Les, but an association began that was to last for over a decade.

I remember clearly how Derek used to arrive to start work at a time when most people were hurrying home. At AP Films, though, we worked all day and late into the night. We were ridiculously under-staffed and our budget for *Twizzle* was shoe-string. For us there were no union hours and I would often feel weak with fatigue as I determined to keep up with the men. We were all young and building the foundation of a brilliant future, of which the five of us – Gerry, Arthur, Reg, John and myself – had few doubts.

But the way was hard, and we would often leave Derek working until the early hours of the morning, creating his magic and transforming the backdrop into a mystical scene. He would grab four or five hours of sleep and then be at Shepperton by 8.30 a.m. the next morning. He did this for several years until he joined our permanent staff in 1961 for the production of *Fireball XL5*.

Derek had been brought up in an atmosphere of film. His mother had been secretary to the movie tycoon, Alexander Korda and stand-in for Merle Oberon, a big star of the forties and Korda's wife. Derek's father was a master carpenter at Denham Studios, where his wife also worked. He remembers his father making toy guns for him and his brother during the war, when it was impossible to buy such things in the shops. He was apparently an expert and perfectionist from whom Derek obviously inherited his talents, not only as a superb artist, but also as a craftsman of supreme practicality. His mother and stepfather ran a hotel called Denham Court in South Devon and Derek, like so many of our team, attended art school there. After four years, he followed in his parents' footsteps and entered the film industry.

In 1961, by the time we had become involved with ATV and Lew Grade, we had gained enough confidence in our future and financial security to ask Derek to join us full time. In any case it had become impossible to continue with the old arrangement of Derek moonlighting at nights and weekends, and working elsewhere during the day. A backlog of work had built up and we never seemed to be able to catch up. We needed Derek's full involvement and to get it he reminded me that we offered him the princely sum of £20 a week. This persuaded him finally to take the plunge with us and give up his other connections.

We were beginning to be taken seriously by the rest of the industry at last, and, by producing a new series almost every year for Lew Grade, were able to provide almost continual work for our film technicians and puppeteers. Television was still considered the poor relation to film, though, and we were yet another rung lower down the status ladder with our puppet productions. In fact, one of the reasons why we dreamed up the name Supermarionation was to distinguish the pure puppetry of the stage from our more sophisticated filmed-television version.

If Derek considered he had worked hard with two jobs, it was nothing to the mountain of work that he had to tackle with us, now that our productions had become increasingly ambitious. But as I have indicated already he was a man of many talents, and combined with an enormous capacity for hard work, he was well able to cope with the demands of the job. I like to attribute his excellent qualities to outstanding natural ability together with a background knowledge of the film world. He understood the insecurities, the demands and the unpredictability of show business, an appreciation of which can come much harder for others reared in a more conventional atmosphere. Sometimes people with talent simply do not have the aptitude or stomach for the see-saw existence of the film world; it is not even an acquired art, more a reflection of inherent qualities and Derek possessed these to the full. During our slow climb to success, they were appreciated and consolidated.

It was 1961 and we were well into the production of *Fireball XL5*. Derek's role was a major one: he designed the main craft, drew the storyboards (the shot-by-shot illustrations of the scenes, highlighting those requiring special effects), built the hardware, planned the shooting schedule and directed the visual-effects sequences. Grinning at the memory of those days, he recalls that they used to call him the White Tornado and his face lit up at the mention of his colleagues, such as Jimmy Elliott, Shaun Whittaker-Cooke and Harry Oakes. He also remembered his assistant Mike Trim, a brilliant artist, who later designed some of the various secondary craft.

My memories of the special effects (FX) team centre on their great sense of humour and love of their work: nothing was impossible for them, they had endless patience, endless ingenuity, especially for their own amusement, off-camera. Once they built a giant polystyrene nose, not for the series, but for an inquisitive member of the executive staff. Gerry had had the rather grand idea that he wanted an executive assistant, as well as his secretary, Una Parrott, and he found someone who had once in the distant past worked for Alexander Korda. This appealed to Gerry, who appeared to forget that he himself was no Korda figure and that working on puppets was hardly the same as producing Korda's epics. The result was that after the initial novelty wore off, Gerry lost interest in his PA and the poor man was left to his own devices, which meant that he constantly interfered with everyone else, and not least with the visual effects department. He asked questions and generally checked up on what they were doing. Although he was basically harmless and well intentioned, he just did not understand this group of off-beat artists, who vowed that the very next time he asked the question, 'What's that?', they would tell him it was his nose. Once bitten, he left them well alone.

Then there was the time when Lew Grade paid one of his rare visits to the studio with members of the board of ATV. The FX crew were preparing a scene which involved an explosion and in order to get a realistic effect, Derek had placed bags of cement in the rafters. These would burst when the explosion occurred and so Derek had moved Lew and his companions well out of range. One of the board members grew inquisitive and decided to have a better look at something, dragging Lew along, too, in his enthusiasm. Suddenly aware that the shot was underway, and that Lew was under fire Derek tried succinctly to explain the problem. It was too late, however; the take went as planned and the bags of concrete exploded, raining cement dust. Thus the desired special effect was achieved, with the added bonus of covering Lew and colleagues in cement dust from head to foot. The crew collapsed in convulsions, while Lew, to his credit, took it in good part, his hapless companion frantically brushing him down.

After this, we were terrified that our request for a bigger budget would be rejected. Instead they marvelled at the realism of the special effects, while not lingering for new wonders. Studio gossip held that it was one of the crew's infamous practical jokes, but Derek assures me it was an accident and who am I to dispute it?

Derek designed a variety of new craft for our many series, inspired by pictures of the latest machines and aircraft, and by the space-age revolution that was upon us in the early sixties. The design of *Fireball XL5* was based on the Russian vision of a spacecraft that took off horizontally, at a time when all rockets were launched standing on their tails. It would start off on a track and accelerate along that track, until in the take-off position. This development was of interest to Derek and he used it as a model for *Fireball XL5*. He was thrilled with the design, and set about the daunting task of making it work in practice. Derek never began by thinking about the how of design, which would have been too conventional and inhibiting, although he admits to doubts when it came to filming the craft actually taking off from the ramp. All went well until the point at which it had to gather speed and take off. When it failed to defy gravity, the FX team had to use all their ingenuity to get it to launch. Precious time was spent experimenting, but with trial and error their patience paid off. In our miniature world we were out in front of the space race.

During the transmission of *Fireball XL5* in 1963, an article appeared in the *Daily Mirror* headlined: FACT IS CATCHING UP ON SCIENCE FICTION. It read as follows:

> The real-life spacemen are catching up fast with Steve Zodiac and Venus, puppet stars of the TV science-fiction series, *Fireball XL5*.
>
> As every one of the 3,500,000 regular viewers knows, when the *XL5* crew want to investigate some far-off planet first hand, they first put *Fireball XL5* into orbit around it.
>
> Then they make the final descent to the planet from the mothership on a kind of Space-taxi, called *Fireball Junior*. The two are later joined together again for the journey back to base.
>
> And that is the way – United States top space scientists have now decided – the first Americans will descend to the surface of the Moon some time around the end of 1967.
>
> They will use a Space-taxi separated in Moon orbit from the huge Saturn rocket assembly that will lift the explorers from the Cape Canaveral launch pad. Next month, a £120,000,000 contract for the construction of a series of these Space-taxis – probably two dozen – will be signed in Washington.
>
> Officially, they are known as LEMs – short for Lunar Excursion Vehicle – but American Space scientists have already christened them Moon bugs. It will weigh 12 tons when it leaves Earth. A dummy Spaceman stands at the side of the model to give some idea of the size.
>
> When the Saturn third stage rocket, with a three-man crew housed in the 40-ton *Apollo* Spaceship at the front, goes into parking

orbit round the Moon, the Moon bug will be detached for final descent. Then two men will ride in the Moon bug, while the third stays behind in the mothership – just as in *Fireball XL5*.

When the Moon exploration ends, the two men will blast off from the lunar surface, and hook up in orbit with the *Apollo* mothership – JUST AS IN *Fireball XL5* . . .

The other week, Steve Zodiac and Venus had a nasty encounter with a robot Space-bird, invented by scientists on an alien planet . . . United States scientists are to build a Space-bird shortly to be sent into space late next year. It has wings 10 feet wide and a wingspan of 96 feet. The big Space-bird will 'fly' at heights of between 800 and 300 miles for a year.

Purpose – to find out how many times its big wings get hit by meteoroids – particles of Space-debris ranging in size from a grain of sand to rock.

Although I am not sure how many of the above inventions were adopted by the American Space Programme, we were obviously on the right track.

When the time came to design the *Thunderbirds* craft, Derek employed current technology and then took a giant step into the future. This explains why so many of our action sequences are credible years later: we were ahead of our time, not in a pure fantasy, but rooted firmly in a future reality. Surely the art of good science fiction is to make the initial premise credible enough to be accepted by a present-day audience, but also to take it one step further into the future. This was our approach with all aspects of Supermarionation – the sets, costumes, hardware, mise-en-scene – and this goes some way to account for its enduring popularity over twenty-five years.

The *Thunderbirds* craft were a masterpiece of Derek's design and invention. They covered all aspects of security – land, sea, air, space – and each had their own uses and powers. *Thunderbird One*, piloted by Scott Tracy, the eldest son, was concerned mainly with assessing trouble and directing operations. The script called for Scott to be carried to his craft on a moving gantry; an intricate system of moving tracks and ramps carried the giant rocket downwards to the launch pad. Such were the specifications outlined in the bible; all Derek had to do was to make them work!

The script went on to describe the five *Thunderbirds* craft as they would appear each week in the title sequence:

> *Thunderbird One,* the 15,000 mph rocket, comes out of the swimming pool, palm trees swaying and smoke billowing from its tail. *Thunderbird Two* – transporter of the heavy rescue equipment – is housed in a hanger behind a cliff face. It is comparatively slow, travelling at a maximum speed of 2,000 mph, piloted by Virgil Tracy and the 'heavy-duty' arm of the International Rescue fleet. *Thunderbird Three,* the spacecraft, awaits pilot Alan Tracy, down in the heart of Tracy Island. A moving couch descends, transporting Alan to his craft. With a hum of compressed air, it jerks to a halt on a trolley riding on a narrow track. Electrical power floods the circuits, and the trolley is whisked forward to the waiting red giant. The couch halts again and now Alan is thrust upwards, directly into the control cabin of the craft. There is an eruption of sound as three giant engines kick into thunderous life. As they scream louder, the craft begins to shudder, then she is away, roaring through the Round House for the emptiness of space. *Thunderbird Four,* the underwater scout, is carried aboard *Thunderbird Two* and piloted by Gordon, who is also Virgil's co-pilot. Finally, *Thunderbird Five,* the super satellite, appears. Its function is to orbit earth and monitor global communications.

Every week viewers watched this title sequence of the show and we all took for granted the talent, creativity and ingenuity that went into the planning and execution of these shots.

But these title sequences were only feasible after the visual effects team had perfected their shots and got the craft successfully to launch. To achieve this with the usual flair and professionalism that had become the hallmark of Derek Meddings and his twenty-eight man team, they worked on three stages, and took five and a half months to complete all the special effects on *Thunderbirds Are Go!* Each craft was produced in sizes varying from a small Dinky Toy, from six-inch dimensions, to a large seven-foot long model. Each size was used for different shots, and made exactly to suit the particular scale of the sequence. For example, a long shot would require a smaller version of the prototype than close up. Then, too, for sequences involving the actual puppets, all craft would have to appear in exact proportion to the characters, that is one-third of life-size. Separate sections of particular vehicles would be made up for even closer shots, as, for example with Lady Penelope's Rolls-Royce, manufactured in at least four different size models, as well as the separate large sections of the car.

To give an example: during the dream sequence involving Alan and Lady Penelope in *Thunderbirds Are Go!*, the pink Rolls-Royce goes into space with Lady P and Alan. In the opening shot the full puppet-size Rolls-Royce (roughly one-twelfth life-size) containing Lady P, Parker and Alan takes off; the scene then cuts to a long shot of FAB 1 in the space sky, quite small in the distance, in model shot (the smallest size) and, yet again, in medium shot as the Rolls comes closer into view; finally the sequence ends at the Swinging Star, space night-club and we now see the scaled puppet-size section for the final arrival shot.

Another scene in the film involves Alan falling from the car and hurtling into space. Once again different size models are required for each scene, not just for Alan himself, but also for the Swinging Star and FAB 1. Everything has to be in exact proportion, which was quite a tedious and painstaking business to organize.

Sometimes it was necessary to use a real-life location as opposed to the studio for a more extensive visual-effects shot, as in filming the craft *Zero X*, in *Thunderbirds Are Go!* The script required that it be filmed in long shot. For this a real-life location – a rather futuristic power station, in fact – around the corner from the Slough studios was used, incorporating the gantry of the power station in order to make the *Zero X* crash appear realistic.

The famous explosions that appeared in every episode of *Thunderbirds* were simulated by remote-controlled electric detonators, which set off cordex explosive (often used by safe breakers). The spectacular explosion called for in the film was achieved by the use of gunpowder, magnesium and petrol gel, suggesting the ignition of gallons of petrol. Incidentally, because of the dangerous materials used, all the visual-effects teams were trained in fire-fighting experience. The magnificent *Zero X* model, specially made for the film, took many weeks to construct and just two days to destroy in various stages.

In order to create the exhaust smoke during take-off of the various craft, custom-made silver metal tubes, filled with compressed gunpowder were implanted in the rockets at the back. Cement dust was also used to create the trail of smoke and the whole thing shot at high speed to slow the action down and create a lasting effect, particularly with the dramatic explosions. The craft were on wires in order to control the action, and operated by a member of the team out of camera range. One of the *Zero X* models was seven-feet long, weighed fifty pounds and cost around £2500 to make in 1966. Having carefully constructed the craft, they would then be dirtied down for the shot and invariably blown up. This never happened, of course, to the *Thunderbirds* craft, which were, for our story purposes, virtually indestructible.

Resourcefulness is the mother of invention in this business and this was apparent in the creation of our models and props. Derek was known to use cigar tubes for some of the rockets and in fact I used to save all Gerry's empty ones for this purpose. Sometimes small manufactured model toys would be utilized – adapted and built on for our purposes. Indeed, there were lots of tricks of the trade that remain just that, but it is still amazing what can be done with string, match boxes and twisted pieces of metal.

A further piece of ingenuity emanated from the special effects department in the making of the Martian Rock Snakes. They sounded good when we wrote them in, but proved quite a challenge to our manufacturing team. Not only did they have to look evil, but they also had to act evil, twisting and uncoiling in snake-like shapes, and then unleashing a fusillade of devastating fire, spitting balls of alien explosive material in the path of the visiting craft. I rather think they used ping-pong balls painted red for their mouths, with rubber, polystyrene and a great deal of green paint to complete the picture.

Fibreglass was in constant use both in the effects department and the puppet workshop. It is an effective, but foul-smelling fabric to which I became allergic; every time I walked anywhere near it, I would break out in a prickly rash. I kept quiet about it as I did not think I would get much sympathy from the puppet- and model-makers, who were working with it all the time. Now, though, it can be told. *Zero X* was made of fibreglass and I kept well away while it was being constructed.

From the days of moonlighting in our cramped, makeshift studio by the river, Derek had become the foremost special-effects director in Britain. Who else had the experience of hands-on production in the world of sci-fi, week after week, year after year? A name that immediately springs to mind, of course, is Stanley Kubrick, director of *2001*. He had eyed our visual-effects team greedily from afar until one day I received a phone call from him, suggesting lunch. He mentioned that he was doing a movie called *2001*, which he would like to discuss with us. Immediately I was put on the defensive: he would not have been the first person to try and poach our staff, especially our star department heads. I agreed to lunch, however, as I was a great admirer of Kubrick's work, his famous anti-war film, *Paths of Glory*, with Kirk Douglas being an all-time favourite of mine. But I was straight with him and warned that we were not interested in loaning out our staff or taking on other people's effects, but if he was still interested in lunch, then that would be fine. There was only a moment's pause before the brusque voice on the other end said that we should forget about lunch, as there was no point now, and my 'hero' hung up. Since then I still consider him a great film-maker, but one very short on charm.

There is a postscript to this story, however, in that he did manage to lure away one of our key visual-effects crew to work on his epic. Fortunately for us, we had Derek Meddings firmly under contract, and beyond the temptations of Mr Kubrick. In those days our *UFO* series could not have competed with his budget.

Prior to this, our second film for the cinema with the *Thunderbirds* series characters and International Rescue was produced in 1976: it was called *Thunderbird Six*, an exciting action-packed story that had some stunning special effects. It also had some real-life drama that ended up in court. In one of the sequences, which involved a Tiger Moth, there was a rescue whereby an airship, designed by Derek like an aircraft carrier, was in distress.

Thunderbird Two was too heavy to implement a rescue, so a Tiger Moth was called in to land on the airship and trawl the crew to safety on each of its wings. The plan was to film real-life footage of a Tiger Moth flying low under a newly constructed motorway bridge, complete with dummies on each wing, and without its wheels touching the ground, taking off again. Derek would then match in his model shots.

The pilot of the Tiger Moth was a lovely woman called Joan Hughes. Quiet, unassuming and highly regarded in her profession, she taught British Airways commercial pilots how to fly light aircraft. She was also highly responsible and, unlike some stunt fliers I have known, took very few uncalculated risks.

We selected a new stretch of motorway that was under construction and not yet open to the public. Various permissions were sought and obtained, and the day of the shoot arrived. Apart from the camera crew, the main unit director and Derek, a Ministry of Transport official insisted on being present. From the start it was obvious that he highly disapproved of the whole caper and was there to see that the rules set out were followed to the letter. Unfortunately, rules are only there to be broken in the film world, and nothing rarely goes to plan or as laid down in the script, especially when on location and outside of the control of the studio. This occasion was no exception: first, a cross-wind had blown up, upsetting the balance of the flying conditions that had, at first, seemed ideal, and second the Ministry ruling was that we had permission to film the shot under the motorway bridge, but that we must first touch down and go under the bridge with wheels down before taking off again.

Joan Hughes listened to her instructions, but doubted, if the wheels were to touch down, that she could get up enough air speed to become airborne again. She was told she had to do it that way or risk getting thrown off the motorway and possibly fined. So several attempts were made to take an exciting shot and stick to the rules, but nothing worked out. The cross-wind was getting stronger, tempers becoming increasingly frayed and the Ministry official growing more officious by the minute. Joan was becoming frustrated by the hidebound rules that stupidly increased the danger from the shot rather than protecting her. But the man from the Ministry was adamant that rules were rules.

The light was fading, the wind blowing stronger and there was time for just one more take. A brief conference was held between Joan, Derek and the director, and the camera started to roll in yet another attempt to capture the shot. Twenty-five years later, it is still not quite clear exactly who said what to whom, but Derek now confesses that he did tell Joan that the previous shots had not been very exciting, and so, with that comment ringing in her ears, what followed was not very surprising. Everyone positioned themselves as the Tiger Moth took off for the final time: the Ministry boffin concentrated hard, determined not to miss a wrong move; the director ordered the cameras to roll; Derek, by his side, tensed as the plane came into shot and did a perfect descent on its approach to the motorway bridge in a clean sweep under the bridge without touching the ground and away.

This was exactly as scripted and beautifully executed, and the crew gave an involuntary cheer. In their enthusiasm, though, they had totally forgotten about the presence of the irate official, who was, by now, jumping up and down in fury on the motorway verge. He vowed on the spot that such a flagrant disregard of the rules would be punished, and he was true to his word: Joan Hughes received a court summons, together with our film company, by then called Century 21 and represented by Norman Foster, the production manager. Fortunately, all fourteen charges were dropped against us, much to the frustration of the over zealous official, and Joan Hughes was so respected in her field that her explanation of the situation was accepted totally. She maintained, quite rightly, that she would have been in more danger if she had complied with the official's rules than by making her own judgement.

Although we were relieved by the court's decision, there were still problems because all the motorway shots had not yet been filmed. The court case had put everything on hold. Derek therefore had to complete the sequence using model shots. In a follow-up scene where the Tiger Moth had to bounce along the motorway, he spent six weeks in a field, with a reconstructed motorway bridge and two radio-controlled Tiger Moth models, specially built by the effects department, each with five-feet wing spans. There was also a 300-feet run of motorway and bridge to set up, with background to match the live-action shots. But the sequence proved to be as troublesome with models as it was with the real thing: the remote-control planes were fine when they were flying but on landing they slewed all over the road. Eventually, after endless takes, Derek settled for a very exciting shot, whereby the model craft bounced across the central reservation. This gave the sequence an excitement which could never have been achieved with the real thing. The result was a stunning highlight to the film, but at what cost the audience would never know.

One of my favourite episodes of the *Thunderbirds* series was 'Attack of the Alligators', written by Alan Pattillo and directed by Dave Lane. It was quite brilliant and had terrific atmosphere, reminiscent of the Bob Hope classic, *The Cat and the Canary*. This was not a Lady Penelope adventure, as was usual with Alan's stories, but, in my opinion, it was still one of the best. As always, the script was ambitious to say the least, and this time required live alligators, just to add to the usual problems. What we used were crocodiles who arrived with their handler from the North of England.

Once more, Derek was thrown in the deep end, only this time literally so. He had designed a huge watertank for *Stingray* in 1963, built in two sections with centre clamps. This was recycled for use in this episode and Derek and his assistant spent most of the picture in the tank wearing high waders, out of camera range, of course. One particular shot had to be a close-up of the crocodile's head, just breaking water, glaring at the boat ahead of him and then finally opening his jaws menacingly. To achieve this, Derek, with the handler, had attached the crocodile to a specially made wooden frame, which could pull the animal towards the camera in order to get a shot. The crocodile at some point broke loose and I have never seen Derek move quite so fast in his life as he did out of that tank. Panic ensued as the handler recaptured the reluctant star.

The shot proved increasingly problematic when the recaptured crocodile just refused to open its mouth at all: there was simply no menace about it. During a hurried conference with Derek and the handler about how to persuade it to open its mouth, someone suggested applying a mild electrical charge of some twelve volts. The handler agreed that it would do no harm: no worse than an electric fence for sheep, he reasoned, but he had reckoned without the reptilian thick skin and the crocodile simply did not react. After a further conference, the voltage was increased and this time the jaw opened and snapped shut as the cameras rolled. Of course, we did get a visit from the RSPCA, tipped off by an anonymous phone call, but they agreed that no harm had been done and spent the rest of the day watching the reptiles at work. All in all, there was much relief when the picture came to an end: temperamental crocodiles were a new hazard and one not to be repeated.

When I met Derek, he paid a special tribute to lighting cameraman Harry Oakes for all his good humour and patience during the years of visual FX filming. Nothing was impossible for this skilled man and it is no surprise that he went on to work on some major film productions, such as the recent *Memphis Belle*. Derek, too, has had a brilliant career, working on five James Bond movies and winning an Oscar for his work on *Superman I* and a BAFTA award in the eighties for visual FX. He also received an Oscar nomination for *Moonraker*. When he attended the Oscar ceremony in Hollywood it was like a dream come true for him. As he and his wife

Above: Hank Marvin and Brian Bennett of The Shadows with me on the set of *Thunderbirds Are Go!*

Left: Directing Cliff Richard, bursting into song.

Right: Visual effects director, Derek Meddings, and production manager, Ken Holt, in model workshop, Slough . Studios.

Far right: Wardrobe mistress, Iris Richens, discussing 'limbs' with me!

Below and below right: The finishing touches for visual effects on *Thunderbirds*.

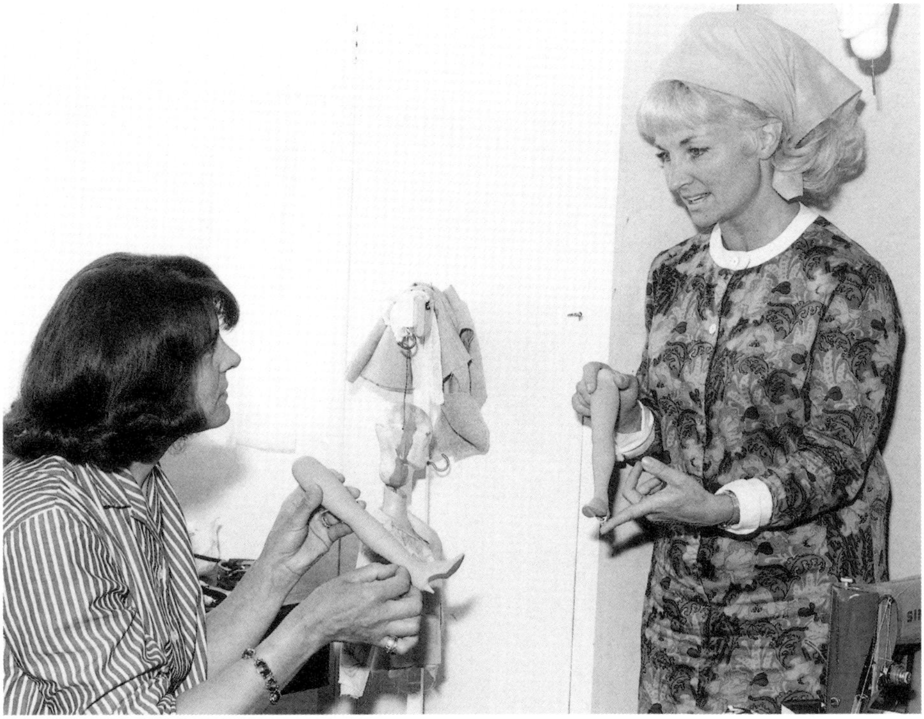

Above: The Martian Exploration Committee. *Right*: Lady P and Alan Tracy at The Swinging Star nightclub. *Far right*: Lady P disguised as singer Wanda Lamour.

4
THUNDERBIRD
4
PENELOPE
CHOOSE A NEW NAME

Top left: Co-directors, Reg Hill, myself, Gerry, and John Read at the Slough Studio in 1965. *Far left*: Gerry and myself showing off the puppets. *Above*: The hazards of making *Thunderbirds*. *Left*: Director, David Lane, and visual effects director with me, Alan Tracy and TinTin.

Overleaf: A small selection of the many products inspired by *Thunderbirds* in the sixties.

THUNDERBIRDS

THUNDERBIRDS STENCIL SET

THUNDERBIRDS
Plasticine

MERIT THUNDERBIRDS INTERCOM SET
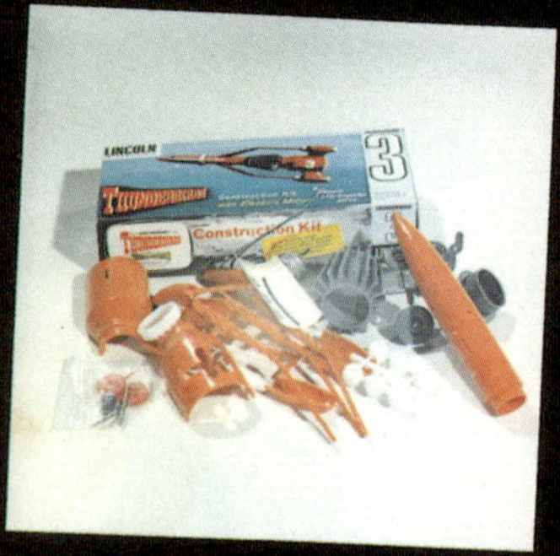
LINCOLN
3
THUNDERBIRDS
Construction Kit

THUNDERBIRDS
GIVE-A-SHOW
PROJECTOR
5 4 3 2 1

WADDINGTON'S
THUNDERBIRDS
GAME
A UNIQUE TYPE OF TEAM GAME
5 4 3 2 1
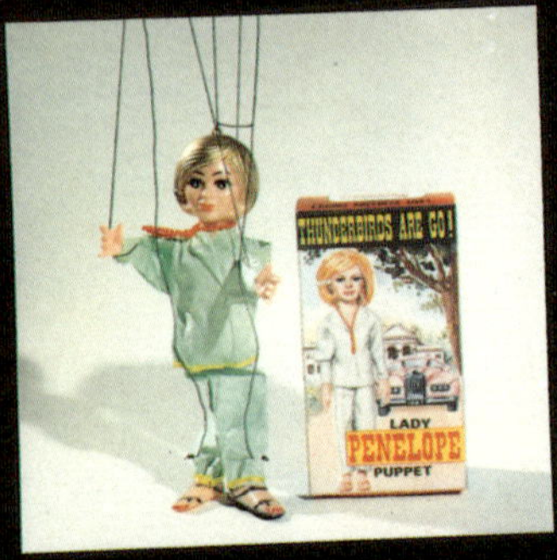
THUNDERBIRDS ARE GO!
LADY
PENELOPE
PUPPET

Kellogg's
SUGAR SMACKS
Thunderbird 2 to Control
Sugar Smacks are GO
THUNDERBIRDS
CUT-OUTS

Lyons Maid
ZOOM
Lyons Maid
CREAM
ZOOM
6d
Lyons

THUNDERBIRDS
3d
NOUGAT
THUNDERBIRDS
NOUGAT
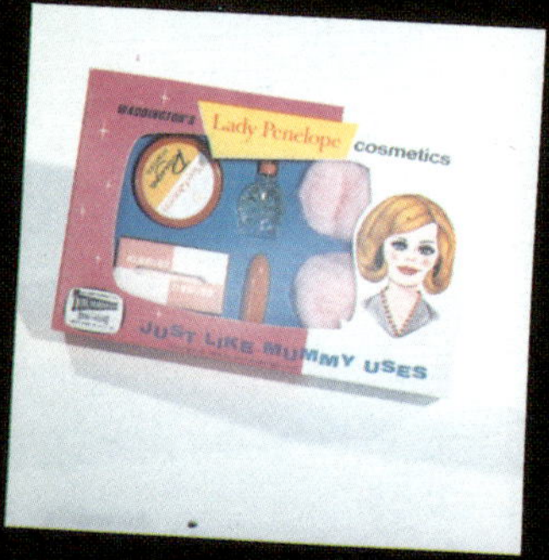
WADDINGTON'S
Lady Penelope
cosmetics
JUST LIKE MUMMY USES

LADY PENELOPE
Elegance Charm and Deadly Danger

Lady
PENELOPE
ANNUAL
THUNDERBIRDS
ANNUAL

climbed out of their limousine and walked along the red carpet, a cheer went up and he half-joked with his wife that the crowd recognized him. His moment of fame was shortlived though when he looked over his shoulder and saw that the cheers were for John Travolta. It was still, for him, a nice moment.

On the topic of awards, it is interesting that, considering our commercial success, we received comparatively few awards from our peers in the film and television world. We did get the Silver Medal for Outstanding Achievement in 1966 from the Television Society for our work to date and *Thunderbirds* in particular, which was a very prestigious award for us. This was rare recognition, however, of the marvellous visual effects that were produced week after week. Invariably we received public acclaim when they were given an opportunity to vote for their favourite programmes, but the industry itself did not hand out many bouquets. This was partly, I suspect, because our type of programmes were rather looked down on as children's programming and biased towards an American audience.

Lew Grade had problems with this perception, too, even though the programmes that he financed were sold all over the world and won him the Queen's Award for Industry. Gerry and I even heard in 1967 that because of the value of our programmes overseas, we might receive an MBE and we supplied the details as requested but never heard any more. We were also invited to the Royal Garden Party that same year, in recognition of our contribution to film exports, but I was forbidden to attend on doctor's orders as the birth of our son was imminent. I, of course, wrote to Buckingham Palace, explaining the reason I could not attend and asking to be invited the following year. It was strictly against protocol and, disappointingly, I was never asked again. But I can say that I was almost there!

Both Derek and I agreed that our programmes were forerunners to the movies of Lucas and Spielberg, but unfortunately for us perhaps a little ahead of their time, as with *UFO* and *Doppelgänger*, which we made after *Thunderbirds*. *UFO* was not the commercial success that everyone had envisaged. Sci-fi subjects were associated with low-budget 'B'-pictures in 1969 when the series was made, and rarely attracted top star names. I am still very proud of *UFO*, and it has since built up a strong cult following, but I believe some of the scripts could have been stronger. Recently though I saw one of the episodes at a retrospective of our work and was agreeably surprised at its production and entertainment value. I think that *UFO* is on course for a revival and believe the series will stand up well after twenty years.

Doppelgänger was based on an interesting premise of a duplicate earth, a *doppelgänger* concealed behind the sun. It was our first big-budget, live-action film, made in 1968 and directed by Hollywood veteran, Robert Parrish. It also had a science-fiction theme, inspired by a story that Gerry and I had written some time before and tucked away in a drawer.

One day, during an ATV lunch at Elstree, Jo Douglas, then Head of Drama, asked me if I had anything suitable for the Plays of the Week slot. I promised to look through our files and in doing so discovered *Doppelgänger* in story form. Having read it through and decided it was too good for a television play, I suggested to Gerry that we try to develop it as a movie. This is what happened and we worked on the script with Donald Robertson, the co-writer, and set it up with funding from Universal and Lew Grade. Being our first live-action movie, there were quite a few teething problems, but the visual effects that Derek produced are some of the finest we ever did. One sequence, in particular, when I saw it in rushes, convinced me that it was a real Cape Kennedy launch shot. Although I was used to seeing model shots, this one, even without sound, defied belief, which is a great compliment to Derek and his team. I saw the film a few years later on television and was still impressed by the magic of the effects. Technology has come a long way since the early seventies, but Derek's effects have endured.

With *Doppelgänger*, we won an award in the United States for the best sci-fi movie on release in 1970. American audiences and critics were much more receptive to our first live-action movie; they had not, as much as British reviewers, related to our work in Supermarionation. It was all too easy to compare our real actors with our puppet characters and descriptions such as wooden, expressionless and puppet-like were cheap shots some of the UK critics could not resist. It was particularly hard on such fine actors as Herbert Lom, Roy Thinnes (of *Invaders* fame) and Patrick Wymark. But it was the price we had to pay for daring to change course and come out of our cosy Supermarionation category. Type-casting is the lazy man's friend, and, boy were we type-cast in Britain.

One element that remained consistently popular in *Thunderbirds* was

Lady Penelope's Rolls-Royce. FAB 1 has become a legend over the years; it was designed by Derek Meddings and approved by the Rolls-Royce company, the famous grille of RR also featured each week in the titles sequence of *Thunderbirds*.

The colour pink chosen for her Ladyship's car was probably my influence and the number plate, too, being an abbreviation for the sixties buzzword, fabulous. It is as simple as that. We issued an official FAB 1 specification for all our readers of our magazine, *TV 21*.

> Following many requests to *TV 21* asking for details of Lady Penelope's Rolls-Royce, the Editor has finally secured permission to reveal some of the interesting features which have hitherto remained TOP SECRET.
>
> The design of FAB 1 has been officially approved by the Rolls-Royce Company, but its main power unit must remain on the classified data list. Speeds in excess of 200 m.p.h. have been attained but it is certain that this is only a modest estimate of the engine's real potential.
>
> The four front wheels have been incorporated in the design to support the weight of the power unit and also the heavy machine guns which are retractable and ready for use at the push of a button.
>
> The car has no driving mirror but relies on a small television monitor screen on its dashboard which receives a television image from the camera concealed in the boot.
>
> Normal television transmitters and receivers, plus UHF and Neutroni radio units are installed within the completely air-conditioned car for immediate contact to and from the vehicle.
>
> When FAB 1 parks all six wheels rotate until the car is able to drive into its parking space sideways.

There then followed a list of extras to the standard car.

> Swivel laser beam and smoke-making apparatus, set in rear wings.
> Rear Hydrofoil.
> The hub-cap motif extends on rod to form a tyre slasher.
> Retractable studs for snow and ice.
> Centre pull-down arm rests have retractable handcuffs and chest band.

Hydraulic platform with fold-down safety rails.
Gull wing canopy and down-and-under doors.
Laminated anti-glare, bullet-proof glass and steel canopy.
Retro pack air brakes.

Hydrofoils when fully lowered extend below level of wheels, thus lifting whole car clear of water when at speed – minimizes resistance. The rear 'foil' has a vortex-aquajet powerpack fitted centrally.

As for Parker and his uniform, an amusing incident occurred when our personal driver was outfitted by me in a Parker-type uniform. He was very proud of it until someone mistook him for a zoo keeper. I was taking care of my parents' pet monkey while they were on holiday. It escaped and was found eventually after all sorts of mischievous exploits, including holding up the traffic on a main road and stealing the cream from bottles of milk. I sent our 'Parker' around to the house where they had Billy the Monkey safely trapped in their dustbin. When he arrived they asked him if he was from the local zoo, on account of his uniform. Somehow, he never felt quite the same again about his futuristic outfit.

If the dialogue is scrutinized in *Thunderbirds*, it is rare to find either Lady Penelope or Parker referring to the Rolls as anything but FAB 1 or the Rolls-Royce. This was in response to the Rolls-Royce company's request not to use an abbreviated description of the car. We knew how to pay the proper respect too. Whatever size model was used for our productions, they were immaculate and perfect in every detail. The life-size Rolls was really a mock up, not a Rolls at all, but a fibreglass shell over a conventional car. It was arranged for this life-size mock Rolls to take us to the première of *Thunderbirds Are Go!*, but we only got a few yards before it unceremoniously seized up and refused to budge. Real life rarely imitates the fantasy world of Supermarionation. We continued our journey to the theatre in a less impressive black taxi-cab.

Bob Bell, our Art Director, had been with us since 1957 when he had assisted Reg Hill with the sets for *Twizzle*. During the *Thunderbirds* era he had an excellent crew and two first-class assistants: Grenville Nott and Keith Wilson. Keith's forte was modern and bold design, with an outrageous use of colour. In 1974 he was to create some fantastic sets on our live-action production, *Space 1999*, for television.

Bob's was no easy task with the one-fifth life-size sets, and he had to work closely with Derek Meddings and the visual effects department. This was necessary in order to match the interiors of the various craft with Derek's overall design. There was often, in fact, some friendly friction between them. Bob had limitations imposed upon him by a very strict series budget and while the exterior of a sophisticated, futuristic design would be possible with a small model used for effects shots, it was more tricky to match the interior with an equally complicated puppet set. Not only did he have to watch the pennies, but also to take into account the puppet movement and shooting requirements. These were different from the problems faced by the visual effects team. While Bob was painfully aware of his modest budget and would try to keep the set design within that limit, Derek would constantly push for a more extravagant match to his exteriors. Somewhere, at some point, a compromise would be reached, that hopefully pleased everyone.

When it came to making the movie, *Thunderbirds Are Go!*, a more generous film budget enabled us to spend a little more time perfecting the art of Supermarionation. Gerry and I once more collaborated on the screenplay, and there was a good balance of character action and visual effects. With the extra money available, the art department was able to design more extravagant sets. The dream sequence, for example, with Cliff Richard and the Shadows was a sheer indulgence that would not have been possible on our television budget. An elaborate set was also written in for the Swinging Star night-club and a giant guitar required construction for the Shadows. I was determined to match the stunning visual special effects, that I knew Derek would provide, with equally striking sets and puppet wardrobe. All this meant that poor Bob had not only the effects department with which to contend, but now also additional pressure from me.

Mostly, though, the art department was given a free hand within its budget, but on one occasion I had very definite ideas about a particular set. I had scripted an ultra-modern conference room for the top officials of the Martian Exploration Project around which the film is based. There were very definite ideas about the design of the room: it had to be in only two colours, tangerine and black, and the puppets would be dressed in a contrasting blue uniform for colour relief. Bob was sympathetic to this proposal and agreed with the visualization. But during the construction of the set, every time I walked on stage I discovered that someone had broke the two-colour scheme. I had to insist on just tangerine and black, continually assuring them that it would look effective. As producer, I was entitled to do it my way and, although I do not think Bob ever really approved, I stuck to my concept. The result was quite a stunning sequence that stood out for its simplicity and economy of colour. I never for one moment doubted that it would work; it was my mental picture and I was in the fortunate position of not having to compromise. For a while, though, I am convinced that the art department thought I had gone too far.

Another aspect of the art department was the props division. All props had to be specially made for the puppets. There was no prop store to hire from, as is normal in a conventional production. Where could one find the right size silver teapot for Lady Penelope; the right size cups, telephone, furniture, bags, pictures, books and all the other props necessary for the sets? Each one had to be carefully scaled down to match the mini world and this is the moment to introduce briefly Arthur Cripps, our property master.

Arthur had arrived to upholster some of our prop furniture. He was a chirpy, local man who loved his pint and game of darts in the pub. Extremely talented and quite unused to the craziness of the film world, when we offered him a full-time job in our props department, he really did not know what to make of us all. He had been recently made redundant from his firm and seemed quite unaware of his talents. We rather took him under our wing and he responded with great enthusiasm; I would like to think that we made the last years of his life happy and fulfilled.

On the day he arrived, he was invited to see the rushes (or dailies as they are called in the States) – the filmed footage shot the previous day. He looked at me suspiciously with his birdlike expression, screwed up his face in distaste and declined. I realized later that he just did not understand what I had meant by the word 'rushes'. Whatever he thought I meant, Arthur soon got into the spirit of things and was thrilled to see his prop creations on the screen. After this he was always first in to see the rushes. He stayed with us until the end of his life, a much loved and valuable contributor to our success.

6

THE CASTING COUCH

Our production company always had an excellent cast of actors who played the voices of the puppet characters. For both the *Thunderbirds* series and films, we used some regulars, like David Graham and Ray Barrett. They had played characters in our early series, David as far back as *Four Feather Falls*, playing the Mexican bandit, Fernando and Grandpa Twink, and then on to Dr Beaker and Mitch the Monkey in *Supercar*. He played another professor in *Fireball XL5* – Professor Matic – and another animal (from outer space this time), with the voice of Zoonie. Ray Barrett joined us on *Stingray*, playing Commander Shore and the villain, Titan.

Thunderbirds had them both speaking in even more voices: Ray, the voice of John Tracy and the Hood; David, playing Brains, Kyrano and, of course, the much loved character, Parker, whose voice has attracted much comment over the years. There is a story about it that is worth recall.

Gerry and I used to eat out in a lovely country pub in the village of Cookham in Berkshire. The waiter there was a real old-retainer type, whom I shall call Albert. Very florid of complexion and very slow and deliberate in his speech, nothing could hurry him. He took a liking to us and would shuffle over to our table at every opportunity muttering about the things he could tell us about the old Prince of Wales (not the present one, I hasten to add). He never got any further than that even; though I eagerly awaited the next titbit of Royal gossip. I would encourage him, but conveniently he would shuffle off to another impatient table and keep me guessing. I never did hear the rest of the story.

During the course of the meal, Albert would become increasingly flushed and beads of perspiration would trickle down his face, dangerously close to the soup! Then his 'Hs' would become misplaced; he would drop them and add them on in all the wrong places. He was, we decided, the perfect role model for Parker and we invited David Graham to study at first hand his perfect cockney voice. It all worked wonderfully well and the voice and character have many imitators to this day: ''Ome, M'Lady?'/'Home, Parker' has become a well-known catch phrase.

Lady Penelope's voice was based on a combination of the actress Fenella Fielding and the late, great Joan Greenwood. When I played her, I loved the husky timbre that took it away from my own voice, giving a distinctive quality. Over the years I had played a variety of voices in our various series: Jimmy in *Supercar*, American ladies in general, Venus in *Fireball XL5* (a sexy continental voice) and, later, in *Captain Scarlet*, one of the Angels (Melody). Then on a more homely note, I voiced Mrs Harris in *Joe 90* and the lovely housekeeper, Mrs Appleby in the *Secret Service*, which was the last of my Supermarionation voices. I am still asked to voice Lady Penelope quite often for commercials. Parker tells me that there is an imposter on the loose who occasionally uses my voice, but he says, 'There's nothing like the real thing, M'Lady!'

Bob Monkhouse was another one of our guest voices, a regular visitor to the studio with our resident actor/voice artist, Shane Rimmer. He was also a great friend of Tony Hawes, a talented, quick-thinking scriptwriter, who worked on many variety programmes, including Des O'Connor's highly popular, weekly show. When I spoke with Bob recently, he reminded me of some of the stunts that Tony had written in to Des's series, in particular a rather *risqué* bathroom sequence. Des is taking a bath when suddenly *Stingray* appears from under the water, between his legs, aping the title sequence of *Stingray* when the craft emerges from the sea. There was some dialogue with his wife in another room that made it a very funny sequence as well as being topical!

It was no surprise that Bob remembered the comedy reference to our show. His career as a comedy writer started back in the fifties with his highly successful writing partnership with Dennis Goodwin. They wrote for every top American comedian, including Bob Hope and Jack Benny. Bob is multitalented and during the *Thunderbirds* era he was as busy as ever with his stage, television and writing projects.

I first saw Bob on the stage in the American comedy, *Come Blow Your Horn*. He was one of the few British artists who could realistically play an American. I mentally noted that he would be good for our cast of transatlantic puppet voices and managed to book him for *Thunderbirds*. His effortless American accent was very welcome to me. Mostly I used Canadian or Australians to play the main roles, since we needed a universal appeal for world-wide sales.

Bob was among many other celebrities to attend the première of *Thunderbirds Are Go!* He was thrilled to be asked to play guest parts in the film and I remember well his enthusiasm and professionalism. As a result of working on *Thunderbirds*, Bob was approached for a guest role in *Crossroads*, another ATV family show.

Apart from Bob's work connection with ATV, there is also a family one. His brother had not shared his ambition to be a performer, and trained as a chartered accountant, eventually working for ATV and Lew Grade. Bob smiles broadly at the thought of his brother signing his pay cheques.

Ray Barrett was part of an influx of Australian actors who poured into London in the sixties. Earls Court was another Oz colony with the likes of Ray, Barry Humphries, and an old-established actor called John Tate. I found that Australians were very good at playing American voices and were great fun, but they did like their liquid refreshments and were often difficult to prise out of the pub during our short lunch-break. Somehow the recording sessions that I directed were even more entertaining after lunch!

Ray Barrett gave Barry Humphries a run for his money with his female voices, especially when he played a really grand duchess in a *Thunderbirds* episode called 'The Duchess Assignment'. He and Barry were macho-Oz types and it was weird to hear them give their brilliant female impersonations. Ray went on to be a star in the *Power Game* and Barry Humphries found fame with his Dame Edna.

Peter Dynely played the voice of Jeff Tracy and was a real Hemingway lookalike. Larger than life and great fun, he was married to ex-Rank starlet, Jane Hylton, and they became our good friends. Sadly, they both died within a short time of each other, but Peter's voice lives on. Later in *Space 1999* I used John Tate's son, Nick Tate. He was an excellent actor, who eventually tired of walking three paces behind the leads, Barbara

Bain and Martin Landau. He had inherited his father's acting ability and versatility and played many voices in our Supermarionation productions. After John died, Nick returned to Australia where he has continued a successful acting career, as has Ray.

Another Australian who took a guest part in *Thunderbirds Are Go!* was Charles Tingwell, who usually played the part of a handsome doctor in television soaps. For us he played a public relations officer. He too returned to Australia. Paul Maxwell was an American, resident in Britain, who is still appearing in guest parts on television. A handsome, charming man, he played Paul Travers, one of the lead roles in the *Thunderbirds* film. Matt Zimmerman, another genuine North American, played the regular part of Alan Tracy and was a fine musical comedy actor, who starred in many West End shows. Alexander Davion, Neil McCallum, Jeremy Wilkin and the lovely Christine Finn, these fine actors all completed our rep company on *Thunderbirds*. These were happy times and we had come a long way from those early days when, as AP Films in the late fifties, we recorded our shows in the bathroom of the country-house studio. I shall always be grateful for those expatriate Aussies who gave me such a wonderful variety of American voices. What would I have done without them?

7

THE SERIES COMES TOGETHER

The bible would be given to a team of writers who would script the various episodes under the script supervision of Gerry and myself. Because of the specialized type of filming – with the limitations of the puppet action – we would often commission a director to write his own episode. It usually worked well as most of them were ex-cutting-room editors and also appreciated the importance of correct film coverage and the use of cutaway shots to overcome a difficult action. It was often easier to use a director in a dual role, rather than attempt to explain the problems to outside writers, who had no Supermarionation experience. When we found new writers, though, who had imagination and flair for our type of production, we used them quite regularly.

Briefing the writing team also meant giving them a clear analysis of the characters and their role in the new series. It was not always possible in the early stages to recognize star quality in the cast of players, because at the beginning of the series none of the characters would have been made or seen on screen. The back story was, therefore, the only point of reference, apart from the first script written by Gerry and myself.

To elaborate a little more about back story, I remember spending long hours with Martin Landau and his then wife, Barbara Bain, when we were setting up *Space 1999* in 1974. They were helping me to invent their own background as lead characters in the sci-fi series. They had just finished starring in the American series *Mission Impossible* and knew their characters intimately. They were, therefore, sticklers for detail in the new series. Sitting in the luxurious setting of the Polo Lounge in the Beverly Hills Hotel, talking about their fictitious relatives and school-days, stays very clear in my memory.

It seemed a little odd that we should spend so much valuable pre-production time talking about events that we would never see, or hear about, on screen. Yet, it is all part of the method-acting philosophy that has served Martin Landau so well in his brilliant character performances.

In writing about the scripts for *Thunderbirds*, it is vital to highlight the contribution of an ex-cutting-room editor, who became our leading director and writer of the series. Alan Pattillo was a talented all-rounder, just made for our type of production, who understood all its aspects, from the problems of editing to the limitations of puppet action. He also had quite a flair for writing some of the best Lady Penelope adventures, such as 'The Perils of Penelope', in which Lady Penelope investigates the disappearance of a scientist. Alan cast her in a Pearl White role (an old heroine of the silent movies who was always the victim) where she is trapped directly in the path of an oncoming express train. This smacked not of sci-fi, but of cracking old-fashioned adventure. Alan co-directed the episode with another ex-editor, Desmond Saunders. Another Pattillo script, and Lady P adventure is 'Alias Mr Hackenbacker', which blends adventure with feminine charm and style. Brains features heavily as Mr Hackenbacker when Lady P is hijacked in a plane on her way to host a fashion show. In the sixties, hijacking was a newly acquired threat and a writer's fodder for exciting material. The fashion show, when she finally got there, was also an opportunity for Lady P to wear a wonderful variety of *haute couture* outfits.

'The Cham Cham' was both written and directed by Alan Pattillo and again gave Lady P a super-star role. I particularly enjoyed this as I got to sing in a Marlene Dietrich voice when Lady P, posing as a cabaret singer, foils a dastardly sabotage plot by using her singing pitch to upset the ultrasonic device of an American rocket. Alan was nothing if not ingenious.

In 'Security Hazard', another Pattillo script, I play the part of Chip, a small boy who stows away and manages to reach Tracy Island, where he is seen as a security hazard. He is safely returned home by International Rescue who ensure that he is left believing the escapade is a dream. For me, this was reminiscent of my voices in *Supercar*. Alan followed this with 'Give or Take a Million', the inevitable Christmas story that must appear in every series! This time the story concerns a group of bank robbers, who trip an alarm; when they try to hide they are transported mistakenly along with a consignment of toys to a children's hospital. The crooks are captured and a lucky child gets the Christmas of a lifetime at Tracy Island. But the prize for the best script of the series must go to Alan's 'Attack of the Alligators', which rates as a real breakthrough in the Supermarionation blend of puppet and animal-effects action.

Alan Fennell, who was to become the editor on *TV 21* and *Lady Penelope* magazine publications, also wrote several *Thunderbirds* scripts, although, curiously, never any specifically for Lady P. His background was in publishing and writing for comics. Dennis Spooner, Donald Robertson, Tony Barwick and Martin Crump wrote the balance of the scripts which followed the first episode, 'Trapped in the Sky', a story about a bomb placed aboard an airliner. Lady P had only a small introductory role in this, but it was enough to capture the imagination of writers like Pattillo and, of course, our audience.

I worked well with all the writers. Tony Barwick I discovered when his girlfriend sent me a sample *Danger Man* script that he had written on spec. I thought it showed great promise and introduced him to Gerry, who agreed with me; consequently he became one of our resident writers for many years. Dennis Spooner, too, was one of my protégés, but, sadly, he died tragically a few years ago. An ingenious writer, he was also ingenious with his excuses for not delivering his scripts on time: like, for example, the time when the post box apparently caught fire and destroyed the manuscript. He was earning a living as a truck driver when I first met him in 1961 in the days of *Fireball XL5*; later he became a comedy writer with Tony Hancock and had a successful writing career.

Writing for Supermarionation did not attract the literary giants of the day and neither did it warrant that. We were making action adventure, sci-fi, boys' own/girls' own adventures and the worst thing would have been to have taken ourselves too seriously. I sometimes cringe when I see an analysis of our storylines; basically they were fun – good, all-round family adventures. It strikes me that there are too few like them around in the nineties.

In order to enhance the background action, in conjunction with painted backings, a process called back projection is often used. BP, as it is known, can transport the audience to any part of the world – at any time and to any place. The art has been perfected over the years and there is no longer a shaky, unreal look to BP shots, as there is in old movies, before the technique had been as fully developed as it is today. It is achieved by means of a projector with a specially designed gate-assembly, with a rock steady intermittent unit, forward and reverse running, automatic phase synchronization device between projector and camera, all remotely controlled so that both projectionist and cameraman can work in complete unison without the complications of talk-back systems or electrical interlock.

Merely by turning on a small switch, both projectionist and cameraman can see, by a signal light, when projector and camera are in phase and the usually cumbersome method of checking back is dispensed with. Shooting can take place immediately the cameraman sees his signal, thereby saving a considerable amount of film stock and, should a partial retake be required, the cameraman can also run the projector in reverse until the desired sequence is viewed on the screen at full brilliance.

Back in 1963 when this process was described in a trade magazine, it was a revolutionary process which served our productions well. Whether it was the Sahara Desert, a busy motorway or a country road, the foreground action was enhanced by a realistic back-projection scene. There were teething problems, of course, as with every new development, but we were able to overcome them with practice during our weekly output of filming.

Once the film had been shot, the procedure was no different from normal television or film production. We always shot in 35 mm film, reduced to 16 mm whenever necessary, with dubbing and track laying (the addition of sound and effects) carried out in the usual manner. As the cutting-rooms were on the premises at the studio, we were on the spot for rough-cut viewing (the first assembly of the footage) and later versions. We also had the facility for viewing our product on television. This was important as big screen and small screen areas differ and we were always aware of television cut-off when framing a scene. There is also a different technique for composing a shot for the two media: television requires a more intimate view of the scene – more close-ups and fewer long shots, that tend to disappear on the small screen; whereas cinema can tolerate a distant shot which does not get lost to the audience.

Whether shooting with puppets or real actors, the same rules apply for each medium, yet many inexperienced television directors would fail to make an impact on the small screen by overindulging in master shots, that is establishing shots not close to camera. Equally, an overuse of close-ups on the big screen can dilute their impact, as they are best used to emphasize a particular point, and not merely a casual reference. Stage, television and the big screen all have their own tricks of the trade. The big screen requires less emphasis and commands more automatic attention; the small screen is intimate and much more demanding; a stage actor's tricks can be overpowering for the cinema audience and where a minimum is necessary for the ever intrusive camera lens, the stage demands flamboyant gestures, projected voices and extravagant mannerisms.

Our blend of visual effects and puppet action was second to none and came with our vast experience in this field. By the time we made *Thunderbirds*, we had, indeed, perfected the art of Supermarionation.

Barry Gray was musical director throughout our Supermarionation career. We served our apprenticeship together on the early programmes, such as *Twizzle* and *Torchy*. From our initial empathy, I remained constantly amazed by his ingenuity and consummate musical skill. A classically trained musician, Barry had worked in almost every type of entertainment, including being Vera Lynn's accompanist during the Second World War when she sang to the troops. He had also written several children's music books, royalties from which had kept him fed and clothed during lean times over the years.

He suited our type of film production ideally because he had a delightful, child-like quality that was conveyed in his work. It was on his original idea that *Four Feather Falls* was based. When we first met he was already middle-aged and had just survived an unsuitable marriage with a cabaret singer much younger than himself. Outwardly he appeared unaffected by the failure of the marriage and bore no malice to anyone; but, as a sensitive, creative person he was undoubtedly upset by the situation. Our meeting came at a good time for him and he threw himself wholeheartedly into working with us and we became firm friends. I enjoyed our visits to his North London home, which was crammed full of musical instruments and the latest electronic gadgetry: music was truly his life.

Barry was in no way a handsome or dashing character – under

average height, a little overweight, bespectacled – but he was, nevertheless, a fascinating companion, especially on his favourite subject of music. We were, indeed, fortunate to have him as part of our team. It was through him that we met a young Australian agent, newly arrived in England, who represented an unknown Australian singer. He approached us with a view to his client singing the title song for one of our shows, but we were not impressed by the singer and declined the deal. The agent's taste improved much later when he was involved with the Beatles and the Bee Gees; he also became a millionaire several times over. He is, of course, Robert Stigwood. There was certainly no indication then of the success and fame he would later achieve.

Barry had written a fun theme song for *Four Feather Falls* and invited a contemporary popular singer to give his rendition. His name was Michael Holliday and in 1960 he was known as the Bing Crosby of his day. I remember going to the recording session and being struck by the individual quality of the singer: he was pleasant and easy going, yet, just a few weeks later, he committed suicide. Quite naturally that encounter has always remained stamped on my mind. I heard the recording again just recently and it sounded as smooth as ever.

Stingray was a big hit for us, not least because of Barry Gray's beautiful music and theme song, sung by the blond, handsome Gary Miller, a singing heart-throb of the sixties. 'Marina Aqua Marina' remains many people's favourite theme song today; it too has stood the test of time.

It was the Shadows who wrote and performed a special song for *Thunderbirds Are Go!* entitled 'Shooting Star'. Cliff Richard sang on the sound-track and there was also a lovely instrumental number for the dream sequence, dedicated to our heroine and entitled 'Lady Penelope'. The compositions from such a rich pool of talent gave us a strong musical content for the film which suited the big screen. We may have had mini stars, but we had a big accompaniment.

However charming the title songs had been in the previous series, Barry surpassed himself when he composed the strident, exciting *Thunderbirds* march. It suited the subject so well and enhanced the visuals tremendously. It remains today a constantly recurring theme for many important occasions. For the movie, *Thunderbirds Are Go!*, Barry recorded the sound-track with a seventy-piece orchestra and his own electronic effects. The result on screen was stunning and elevated our puppet performers into the mega-star bracket, to provide an apt tribute to the memory of its composer.

There were over thirty recordings made of the *Thunderbirds* music and cast, including versions as diverse as Cliff and The Shadows; the Billy Cotton Band; the Netherlands Royal Air Force Band; the Metropolitan Police Band; the Joe Loss Orchestra. I recorded seven *Thunderbirds* records in all, narrating and singing as Lady Penelope; this included a sultry version as a night-club singer in 'The Cham Cham'. It would seem the public could not get enough of *Thunderbirds*.

We had previously had some success with recordings from *Stingray* and *Supercar*, including an arrangement by Nelson Riddle and his celebrated orchestra, who are best known for their work with Frank Sinatra. But nothing compared with the sales generated by the music from *Thunderbirds*. The recent remix of the original themes written by Barry Gray for *Thunderbirds* proves that the public still has a fascination with the classic series; the up-beat version with Parker went to number six in the charts. There is no doubt that Barry Gray made an enormous contribution to our Supermarionation successes and we were very fortunate to have known and enjoyed his enormous talent.

8

CREATING THUNDERBIRDS MEMORABILIA

The history of the merchandising and marketing industry that grew up from our various series dates back to the arrival of Keith Shackleton in 1960. An old friend of Gerry's – they served together as national servicemen in the RAF – Keith was business manager for a company that organized industrial exhibitions around the world. He had just returned from a British trade fair in Moscow when I first met him, during a rather hair-raising drive to London with him to meet Gerry at the Brevet Club in London's Mayfair. I liked him immediately and was pleased when he accepted our invitation to join AP Films during the making of *Supercar*. At that time, only Disney had ventured into the big league of character marketing, which involved a well-known television or film character and the issuing of licences to reproduce toys, books, clothing, or any other by-product based around the character. The United Kingdom lagged behind in the exploitation market place, and in the sixties we were the pioneers in this area.

When Keith became Director of Marketing and Merchandising for us he did not have an easy task. First, our puppet programmes had not yet built up the vast and ultimately exploitable following that resulted later. While we had fans among our audience, some of the reviews were lukewarm, if, indeed, the critics deigned to review us at all. Puppetry, even as advanced as ours, was still placed in the same category as Punch and Judy or arty marionette shows. We lost out too among the purist puppet circles, where our film techniques were much frowned upon. We were at the vanguard of a new technique and as always there was resistance to a new and fairly untried area. Although we were making inroads, the breakthrough had not yet happened and it was against this background that Keith set about creating a marketing plan.

Fortunately, he was able to exploit a situation whereby he made a valuable acquisition for Century 21. In order to build a foundation on which to operate, Keith needed products other than those based on the company's in-house projects. It was during a trip to New York in 1961 that Keith discovered that ITC – the distribution arm of ATV – wrongly believed that they had the American merchandising rights to our current series, *Supercar.* In fact, in our contract with ATV, who had financed the series, these American merchandising rights had not been included. On discovering this, Keith promptly took *Supercar* to a leading American merchandising company, Weston, and placed the US marketing rights with them. He not only did this, but also acquired the rights from them to the television series, *Dr Kildare.* In fact, it was a trade-off and a valuable one at that: *Dr Kildare* became a highly popular television show in the United Kingdom and was a real coup for Keith. So, we were now in the enviable position of launching *Supercar* as a marketing entity in the United States (from which we received a licence fee), as well as having a prestigious American show on which to build a marketing campaign in the United Kingdom.

This all marked the beginning of a highly successful and long relationship with Weston Merchandising, owned by Stan Weston. Weston's fame sprang from the creation of a character called GI Joe, which had phenomenal success and made Weston Merchandising the leading merchandising company in the United States. By the time *Fireball XL5* was in the pipeline in 1961 our marketing arm was well and truly extended. With further vital acquisitions such as *The Man from UNCLE* and *How the West Was Won,* we were well on our way to success with what was to become known as Century 21 Merchandising.

Despite the fact that Arthur Provis had left the company and had been one of the original founder members, we had still kept the name AP Films. Keith suggested, however, that it was time to give our group of companies a more dynamic title and it was he who came up with Century 21 Productions. It had a good ring to it and after a little discussion we adopted it as our new name in 1962. To add to our fast-growing group of companies, we formed Century 21 Records, in partnership with Pye

Records, part of the ATV group. The *Supercar* and *Fireball XL5* theme songs were on the new label and proved extremely popular; when later we added *Thunderbirds*, it proved a phenomenal success. During 1966 and 1967, over twenty-two records issued on the Century 21 record label featured *Thunderbirds* music and cast. I personally received a Silver Disc for the sale of over a quarter of a million records, playing the part of Lady Penelope. There was no doubt about the popularity of the series from a merchandising point of view and the decision to form a joint record company had proved to be totally justified.

Within three years by 1964, Century 21 Merchandising had become a fast-growing empire and by the time *Thunderbirds* had been conceived, we had become officially part of another much greater empire: Lew Grade's ATV. Lew had charted our success and astutely recognized the potential of our programmes and their marketing possibilities and finally he made us that offer we could not refuse. Being the super salesman that he is, he wooed us with an attractive proposition, which, although tempting in its security, also meant the loss of our full autonomy. We had fought hard to be free to make our own decisions and were used to being our own bosses, but we also realized that if ATV withdrew their financial support – as Granada had done earlier – we would be back on the route of money raising, at times a hard and stony road.

Coincidentally, at the same time as we received an initial offer from ATV in 1964, we were also propositioned by a giant of the advertising world, no less than Pearl and Dean. Ernest Pearl had spotted us as a consequence of our highly successful Blue Cars commercial with Nicholas Parsons for which we won top television awards. I am not convinced that Lew Grade believed us when we told him we had another offer we could not refuse, and I think at that time he figured we had invented another mystery bidder. Of course, we were not at liberty to reveal the name of the other party, but, because it was the truth, we were able to bargain from strength.

Although we did contemplate seriously a merger with Pearl and Dean (or should I say takeover?), I think we always favoured the flair and flamboyance of Lew Grade and ATV. It was still a nail-biting time, though, when we indicated to Lew that we would only go along with his deal with some modifications, as well as an improved financial arrangement. He acknowledged our comments and then left us guessing for what seemed like an age and, in retrospect, was probably less than a month. We agonized over what would happen if we lost both deals and slid back to the bad old days. Gerry and I took a well-deserved break from filming in France, after much urging from me, and on our return, we attended an awards dinner given by the *Daily Mirror*. The silence of waiting for a decision from ATV was broken when we met Lew at the reception and he muttered something about seeing us next week. We enjoyed our evening a lot more after that and did come to a mutual agreement whereby we became officially part of the ATV group. For a long time after this we had the best of both worlds: financial security and creative freedom. Lew Grade had been as good as his word.

Our series *Supercar*, *Fireball XL5* and *Stingray* had been featured as strip cartoons in a magazine called the *TV Comic*. They had proved extremely popular and the assistant editor, Alan Fennell, had also previously written scripts for us. As there was a good rapport between us, Keith and Alan began to discuss joining forces on a new publication to be called *TV 21*, to include all our series to date, including the current series, *Thunderbirds*. Century 21 Publishing was about to be added to our group of companies.

Already we had a good relationship with City Magazines, headed by Clive Carr, whose family publishing empire included the *News of the World* (later to be acquired by Rupert Murdoch in consequence of a takeover bid by Robert Maxwell), and *Huckleberry Hound* and *Yogi Bear* comics. Keith discussed the idea of launching *TV 21* with Clive and received a positive response. As we were now part of ATV, the matter had to be discussed first with Lew Grade and so Keith outlined his proposal to Lew and asked for £30,000 to set up the new publication.

Lew responded by suggesting that Keith should find a partner. He felt that already he had committed sufficient money to our company, and he had still to answer to his board of directors. But he did have the good sense to help us approach the idea from another angle; as Hugh Cudlipp, one of the members of the ATV board, was also on the board of another publishing group, IPC, Lew advised that IPC should be given a chance to partner the proposed new venture.

Although we had a partnership deal in place with Clive Carr on behalf of City Magazines, Keith duly saw Hugh Cudlipp and put the proposition to him. Cudlipp was not overimpressed and had reservations about the puppets and their possible success. Nevertheless, he was prepared to match the City Magazines deal, but not with the same enthusiasm and commitment as Clive Carr. Keith discussed the two offers with Lew, who endorsed the new partnership with City Magazines. The way was now clear for the launch of *TV 21* under the editorship of Alan Fennell.

Keith travelled to Liverpool to press the button on the printing presses for the launch issue. The first run was an ambitious 700,000 copies, some target for a new and untried publication. The first sales figures were awaited with anxiety. Keith roamed all the local newsagents, gloomily noting how many copies were still in stock and wondering if we had bitten off more than we could chew and become too confident in our own products. It was another nail-biting time and failure would have been particularly hard to accept this far along the line as there was now so much at stake. We all spent an uneasy weekend, but by the Tuesday of the following week we breathed a collective sigh of relief. Clive recalls returning from a golf match and seeing schoolchildren clutching copies of *TV 21*; it was a reassuring sight. The sales figures as reported by our circulation director, John Littlejohn, had more than lived up to our expectations – we did, indeed, have a winner on our hands. He and Cyril Smith, the managing director of City Magazines, formed part of our team and shared our celebrations.

The following year, 1965, we launched *Lady Penelope*, a magazine headed by the popular *Thunderbirds* character. The two magazines had an amazing combined circulation of over 1,300,000 copies a week. I wrote a column each week – Lady Penelope Investigates – and got to interview all the celebrities of the day. Holland, too, where our shows were always very popular, had their own edition of *TV 21*, selling over 100,000 copies a week!

One of the many free-gift offers that proved extremely popular was a silver locket, embossed with the Lady Penelope Creighton-Ward coat of arms that slid back to reveal a tiny mirror. While researching material for this book, I spoke to a BBC picture researcher, who said it was one of her proudest possessions at the time – in fact, she still had it tucked away with her *Lady Penelope* annuals. I still have my own original, real silver version, given to me by Clive Carr to commemorate the launch and success of Lady P's own publication. The inscription reads: PRESENTED TO LADY PENELOPE (SYLVIA ANDERSON) 22 JANUARY 1966: ELEGANCE. CHARM. DEADLY DANGER (the family motto of the Creighton-Wards).

I reminded Clive of this when I lunched with him recently at the elegant Park Lane Hotel, controlled by his family, and which he now runs. It would have been the perfect setting for Lady Penelope with its tasteful twenties décor. Just the setting too for our get-together after many years. We immediately re-established the rapport we had shared in those exciting, heady days of *Thunderbirds* in the sixties. Clive's observations about those days were as astute as ever. We discussed the fact that even though Lady Penelope had launched her own publication, the television back-up in the early episodes was almost non-existent. This necessitated rearranging the running order of the episodes to include Lady P's adventures. Out of the thirty-two episodes she appeared in less than half. Her real opportunity came with *Thunderbirds Are Go!*; by then there was no doubting her popularity.

During the *Thunderbirds* era, Century 21 Merchandising opened an office in Hong Kong to co-ordinate the production and buying of a wide range of toys. Alistair Sawrey-Cookson, whose uncle was governor of Hong Kong in the 1930s, was in charge of the Hong Kong office. The first duty of visitors from the United Kingdom, regardless of how tired they might be, was to sign the visitor's book at the Governor's House. This ensured that everybody who was anybody knew you were in town. Another quaint Hong Kong custom was the welcome party at the airport, the size of which supposedly reflected the importance of the visitor, but in reality was more directly linked to a rent-a-crowd exercise.

Japan was also important to us in the sixties. After the United Kingdom, it was probably our most successful market with the *Thunderbirds* hardware proving to be very popular with the large Japanese television audience. In the early seventies we were paid what should have been a compliment by the Japanese, who, without any input from us, produced an animated series, *Thunderbird 2012*. Unfortunately because we no longer owned the copyright – sold in 1964 when Century 21 was taken over by ATV – we had no creative input or final approval. The series was not a success, lacking the charm and magic of the original.

At the height of its success in 1966 Century 21 Merchandising was employing over 200 people in publishing and licensing activities. Among the staff employed was a young New Zealander called Richard Culley, Keith's second-in-command, and today highly successful in marketing the Ninja Turtles campaign. It would appear that his experience with our merchandising company in the sixties was a good training ground for his marketing career. I doubt if he could have got a more extensive one in the United Kingdom at that time.

In the early sixties, when the marketing staff consisted of Keith and a secretary, their office was in Orme Court. The Bayswater address was no ordinary one as it housed some of the currently most talented people in the world of comedy. Roger Hancock, brother of Tony Hancock, had a comedy writers' agency in this lovely old house in West London. On my first visit there, as I drove up to the house I had to brake sharply: something or somebody was lying prone in the road. I jumped out anxiously to find a grinning Spike Milligan dusting himself down. Apparently, this was a regular occurrence and his party trick for arriving visitors. It shocked me to think of the waste of talent if I had run him down, but when I mentioned it, he just laughed crazily at the notion.

I entered the house after this rather nerve-wracking experience and was greeted by an equally nervous-looking Eric Sykes, the brilliant comedian and writer. He was, and still is, extremely deaf and I once spent an evening chatting away to him only to be told at the end of the night that I had been talking into his 'bad' ear! The comedy writing duo, Galton and Simpson (responsible for *Steptoe and Son* and many *Hancock's Half Hour* scripts) were also clients and housed in Orme Court. On another floor was the abundant Hattie Jacques playing out a scene to herself.

On other visits I would see a morose looking Tony Hancock staring into space; just occasionally Peter Sellers would drop in and Johnny Speight would arrive, straight from the pub around the corner, to write another episode of *Till Death Us Do Part.* It was a total madhouse, but one more than touched by genius. Our merchandising office right at the top of the building, with its very correct business chief, Keith Shackleton, seemed totally out of place. At the time I did hear rumours, which Keith denies, that he marked all the spirits in his drinks cabinet: it was apparently just too convenient for the other residents to help themselves when their own supplies ran low.

I came to know and like Roger Hancock, who somehow seemed to keep the whole mad bunch together with his own brand of dry humour and astute business sense. Walking in the shadow of a famous brother was not for him; he was a personality in his own right. In the seventies he formed another company, Roger Hancock Associates, which focused on representing writers, only to sell out later to the by then highly successful Robert Stigwood.

Keith's next address was at the Coliseum, Stoll Theatre offices in Mays Buildings. He thought the address was fine except for Mays Buildings, which looked so ordinary on the letter-head that he set about getting it changed. After endless correspondence with Westminster Council, responding to their ten good reasons why it could not be changed, they finally gave in and renamed it, as Keith had requested, Century 21 House, Mays Court, which is what it remains to this day.

The standard of merchandise for which we issued licences was extremely high. Keith was always highly selective and careful when it came to granting permission to reproduce our characters in book or toy form, and the hundred or so lines that were produced. Cereals, clothes, toys, books, posters: the marketing potential was endless. Keith's job was to acquire revenues through the licence fee charged to each manufacturer or company wishing to exploit our characters in the marketplace. It was important to ensure high quality and good value to the public by means of selecting and vetting would-be licensees before granting and issuing the relevant contracts. I was very protective, too, of the characters' spin-offs. For example, dolls and puppets reproduced had to bear a good likeness to their television counterparts and the quality of the goods had to represent good value for money. In the case of Lady Penelope, I designed a range of clothes and approved the immensely popular dolls that were manufactured by their hundreds of thousands.

Dinky Toys had manufactured over two million of Lady P's pink Rolls-Royce, wearing out two sets of die-cast tools in the process. There was a manufacturing bonanza with whole factories prospering by producing *Thunderbirds* memorabilia. Matchbox Toys, Bendy Toys, all the big toy-manufacturing names of the day were fighting for licences. I was kept busy attending toy fairs and promoting the various lines: merchandise was flooding the market at a breathtaking rate.

Today these items, over twenty years later, are much sought after pieces and change hands at collectors' prices. I am constantly offered thousands of pounds for an original puppet figure; a small Dinky Toy which probably cost just a few shillings could now command hundreds of pounds. Most of my collection has been built up over the years at odd sales and from friends and relatives, but, typically, most of us connected with *Thunderbirds* have very little to show materially for that era.

Keith resigned as marketing chief in 1967, having established a vast merchandising operation. He felt that the original ethos of the Century

21 Club, on which our success had been built, was gone; that the salt had lost its flavour, and although the merchandising boom continued into the seventies, the driving force of the original marketing campaign was no longer there. However, he did reform Century 21 Merchandising in the late seventies with offices at Pinewood Studios. The portfolio of merchandising successes include such names as Abba, the New Avengers, Paul Daniels, and he is currently involved in developing a UK merchandising programme for the World Wrestling Federation of America.

Back in the mid seventies, though, the original Century 21 companies went their separate ways and ATV were on the threshold of their own power struggles.

9

FAMOUS FANS

Fascination with *Thunderbirds* has not been confined just to the general public. There was a stream of celebrity visitors to our studios between 1963 and 1967 during the making of the series. One such famous visitor was the actress, Wendy Craig, star of successful television sitcoms such as *Nanny*, *Butterflies*, *Not in Front of the Children* and *Mother Makes Three/Four/Five*, now all classics of television. Married to talented journalist, Jack Bentley, who was at that time show business editor for the *Sunday Pictorial*, Wendy took time off from her own filming to visit our studios with Jack and her two sons, Alasder and Ross. When I met Wendy and Jack again recently, we talked about *Thunderbirds* and it proved to be a nostalgic exchange of sixties' highlights.

Wendy and her family had followed all the Supermarionation series, but *Thunderbirds* was the one that had really captured their imagination. They told me that the whole family would sit down to watch the shows and that every birthday and Christmas meant a *Thunderbird* book or toy, even to the extent, one wedding anniversary, of Jack presenting Wendy with a coffee-coloured Rolls-Royce, which he nicknamed FAB 1. Wendy and the boys persuaded Jack to use his considerable influence to arrange a visit to the studios and I remember feeling flattered at the time, especially as Jack had access to every top sixties' star for his much admired column. The boys were apparently far more interested in the *Thunderbird* characters, though, than in any movie star!

I used to be concerned that tours behind the scenes might take away the magic on the screen, but Wendy assured me that it was quite the opposite with her boys; they just became more intrigued and marvelled at the techniques. Their only surprise was that the puppets were smaller than they appeared on the screen.

Jack mentioned some of the celebrities he had interviewed in the sixties, like Marianne Faithfull and Mick Jagger at home in their palatial country estate, surrounded by hedges of pot, growing wild. Apparently Mick was also a fan, but I was unaware of this until long afterwards – in 1978, to be exact – when I went to Paris with Harvey Goldsmith, the renowned concert promoter and impresario. We were to meet with the Rolling Stones and discuss their appearance in a film called *Rock On*, which I was involved in setting up.

I had had some experience in trying to pin down rock stars to meetings (including the Beach Boys, who constantly seemed to be in retreat and meditating in some remote part of the world). Harvey and I had been through all this in Hollywood, so I was getting used to the unpredictable world of rock stars. Even so, I was becoming a little anxious when several hours had passed pleasantly at dinner with no sign of the band. We had to return to London the next day and it was crucial for our financial backers that we could confirm the interest of this world-famous group in our project. Around 2 a.m., after the food had long since been devoured and the drink was still flowing, I excused myself, by now totally convinced that the whole trip had been a waste of time. Harvey, however, remained unruffled, still confident that we would get our audience.

I woke from an exhausted sleep to the shrill ring of the telephone. As I reached for the phone I focused my eyes on the clock: it was 6.30 a.m. I was instructed to be ready in fifteen minutes for a car to take me to see the Stones. We went to a recording studio on the outskirts of Paris where they were recording their new album. Once at the studios the red recording light remained on for at least half an hour, until it went off again, and Harvey and I were ushered into the inner sanctum.

Tetchily I made some crack about the all-night wait, but was disarmed totally by the warmth of their greeting. They sat me on a stool and gathered around cross-legged on the floor, like small boys huddled around their teacher. I had prepared my speech about the movie and was about to give them my sales pitch when they began to ask me questions – not about the film, but about *Thunderbirds*. I was amazed, as I had not thought for one moment that they would be remotely interested in my previous working life. In fact, I had been careful not to refer to it when setting up the project as, in my experience, it was too easy to be typecast. Once it was known that I had been involved with *Thunderbirds*, it was always a hard task to convince people that I could do anything else (even though I had produced *Doppelgänger*, *Space 1999* and *UFO* with real actors).

Mick Jagger leaned forward eagerly as I responded to questions about the International Rescue team and Lady Penelope and it was an experience that I shall never forget. They dismissed the movie that I was there to discuss with a suggestion that I should send the script to their agent and an agreement that they would do it if they could. As they knew and respected Harvey, they took his interest to indicate that it was worthy of their consideration. Ken Russell, the proposed director, hardly got a mention; the mini puppet stars were of far more interest to them.

One of the other stars I interviewed for my 'Lady Penelope Investigates' column was Roger Moore, then filming *The Saint* at Elstree. *The Saint* was a popular television show and suited Roger's personality well. We both had the same boss in the form of Lew Grade and as such were part of the large ATV family, which in those days, was a very happy band of television players, although we all still hankered after the big movie break. I was always sending Lew novels that I thought would make good movies – preferably with us making them – but up till then I had not had any success in persuading him that he should venture into the movie world. It was a burning ambition for me, though, as I was a complete movie buff and had a storehouse of acquired knowledge that I was aching to put into practice. I envied my fellow producers who had glamorous stars in their shows; of course, they had problems, but at least they were *human* ones.

When we met that day in 1966 on the set of *The Saint* we were not to know that within a couple of years we would both be filming at Pinewood Studios on adjoining stages. Roger with Tony Curtis in *The Persuaders* and me on *UFO* with real, live actors. There was no hint then that Roger would, one day, step into Sean Connery's shoes as James Bond. This, then, is the intriguing thing about show business: its total unpredictability. Both of us being with ATV meant that we were aware and supportive of each other's work, so the interview we had for my column was relaxed and informal. Roger had a terrific sense of humour, as much against himself as anyone else and he was the first to admit he had been lucky in his career. Basically modest, fame has never been a problem for the Saint and 007.

Tony Curtis had become a fan of our programmes as I learned when I invited him to be my guest on a talk show, *Eleven Plus*, that I hosted with the late Russell Harty in the seventies. After I had written a piece on cosmetic surgery, I brought Tony in to talk about the Hollywood obsession with physical perfection. We had met first when he was filming *The Persuaders* with Roger Moore. I discussed an idea with him then for a film about a group of astronauts who, to all intents and purposes, were on a space mission but who, in fact, had never left earth. It was an interesting psychological drama written by Mike Billington, one of our actors in *UFO*. I thought that Tony would be ideal for the lead and he suggested we meet for lunch. We were filming next door on the second series of *UFO*, so I wandered over on to the stage where he and Roger were playing out a scene. When they finished, we went off to Tony's dressing room for lunch, or so I assumed.

Roger, in fact, gave me a rather quizzical glance – with that famous raised eyebrow – when I told him we were lunching. Later I found out why. Tony was on one of his famous diets and that week, unfortunately for me, it was sesame seed and mineral water. I made some quip about it being strictly for the birds and then I started to explain our story. Tony responded eagerly, and likened the space ship to the womb, with the astronauts as the unborn babies. After that, I must admit, I got a little lost and I learned later that Tony was prone to these flights of fancy. I never succeeded in getting anyone else interested seriously in the idea – not even ATV – but later, a similar idea was made into a movie entitled *Capricorn One*.

My other memory of Tony Curtis is in total contrast to his professional face. I went to his home in London's Chester Square, now the new address of Margaret Thatcher, to discuss the television talk show. I expected a Noel Coward scene of Tony languishing in a smoking jacket on a *chaise longue*. Instead, I found him bathing his new-born baby with such tenderness and care that I was taken by surprise. I had seen yet another, gentle side of a highly complex man.

Tony did appear on my show and was a true professional. He told amusing stories about Marilyn Monroe, whom he loathed (having appeared with her and Jack Lemmon in *Some Like It Hot*) and generally charmed everyone in sight. He had the knack of remembering every technician's name and showed genuine interest in their families and lives.

I once met Prince Charles after a charity concert and was introduced as Lady Penelope. This brought a wide smile to his face. It had been rumoured that our Royal action man had been a great *Thunderbirds* fan, but I was too polite to ask him; Royals have a way of making you tongue-tied, which is quite unusual for me. However, my source close to the Palace assures me that it is true, so I am happy to believe it.

Roger Daltrey, the Bee Gees and Olivia Newton-John all have one thing in common: apart from their music, they are all *Thunderbirds* fans. During one of my visits to our home in Portugal during the sixties, I met Olivia, a very pretty Australian then the girlfriend of Bruce Welch of the Shadows. Gerry had returned to England and I was staying on to write. Bruce, too, had gone home and Olivia and I found ourselves the only occupants in the row of holiday villas. During the next ten days we had a crash course in getting to know each other. It was February and the small town of Albufeira was deserted. The weather too was untypically cold and rainy, every restaurant was empty and there was the usual series of power cuts: all in all, it was not very exciting. I knew very little about Olivia except that she was a singer and recently arrived from Australia, but I liked her immediately and we enjoyed each other's company. She told me of her ambitions to become a star and that she was about to do a film, set up by Harry Saltzman, one of the Bond producers. A group of musicians had been formed specially for the film, which was a rock fantasy with science-fiction elements. It did not sound very promising to me, but I had no doubt that Olivia was talented and would, hopefully, fulfil her ambitions: she had a bright, lively personality and the looks to match. Olivia Newton-John did, of course, find fame in Hollywood and, eventually, another love, much to the dismay of Bruce, who really did help her career in the early days. The Saltzman movie was, as I had feared, a complete failure, but her talent was such that it only delayed her stardom and did not prevent it.

When I last saw Olivia – at the London première of *Xanadu* – she had not changed one bit; she had the same self-deprecating humour and sense of fun, still very much the fresh-faced Australian girl abroad. I am pleased to say that she also found happiness in her personal life which is rare in the Hollywood scene. *Thunderbirds* brought me in touch with many aspiring stars, and I have watched their progress with interest over the years: Olivia is one of the nicest.

Portugal was a marvellous place to be in the early sixties as an escape from the hectic life at home when we were in production. Our schedule was gruelling, as we created and produced a new series each year, which drained us physically and creatively. The moment we stepped off the plane there was that unmistakable aroma of exotic fruits and an air of peace and unsophisticated life-style. Although it attracted a small contingent of British show-business personalities in search of the same solitude, we only socialized occasionally and respected each other's privacy. There was a marvellous sense of freedom in Albufeira, reputed to have the best climate in Europe. It also had miles and miles of stretches of golden beaches – often totally deserted.

At any one time you would see Cilla Black and her husband, Bobby, Eric Morecambe and his wife Joan, Jimmy Tarbuck, Ernie Wise, Cliff, the Shadows. Michael Simkin, the show-business lawyer, who represented Peter Gormley and the Shadows, also represented us, and was a frequent visitor to Portugal, usually wheeling and dealing on our behalf and getting us involved in all sorts of overseas schemes.

At the première of *Thunderbirds Are Go!* in December 1966, we had been presented with a villa in Albufeira by Lew Grade as a reward for our work on *Thunderbirds*. It had been previously owned by a theatrical agency belonging to Leslie Grade, Lew's brother and father of Michael Grade, now chief executive of Channel 4. The villa was in the same block as those owned by Cliff and the Shadows. I was delighted with it and went down to Albufeira to sort out furniture and give it the personal touch. On my return, we received a call from Leslie explaining, apologetically, that some time earlier he had promised the use of the villa later that month to his young singer client, Tom Jones. He explained that Tom had recently had a nose-correction operation and needed a place to hide away until his new profile had settled down. Leslie was a charming and polite man and, of course, we agreed readily to Tom Jones's recuperation for a few weeks in our villa. In any case, this was fine as we had met Tom already in the early sixties when we had tried unsuccessfully to strike a deal with his Svengali of a personal manager, the late Gordon Mills. By way of softening the blow, Leslie had added that Tom was a *Thunderbirds* fan too.

* * *

THUNDERBIRDS
THE BEST WOOL
SEE THE MOST ADVANCED SPACE-CRAFT EVER CREATED!
THUNDERBIRDS

Previous page: The Gala Charity premiere of *Thunderbirds Are Go!*, held at The London Pavilion, 12th December 1967.

Above: With the puppets and craft at the premiere. *Right*: The band of the Royal Marines were also there.

Left: Lady Penelope and Jeff Tracy. *Below*: Gerry and I were greeted by a young fan at Edinburgh Airport during the promotional tour for the film.

Right: Parker in trouble again! *Below*: A Martian rock snake in action. *Below right*: The entire *Thunderbirds* crew at the Supermarionation studios in 1965.

Below: Dudley Moore and Peter Cooke in a *Thunderbirds* send-up in *Not Only But Also*.

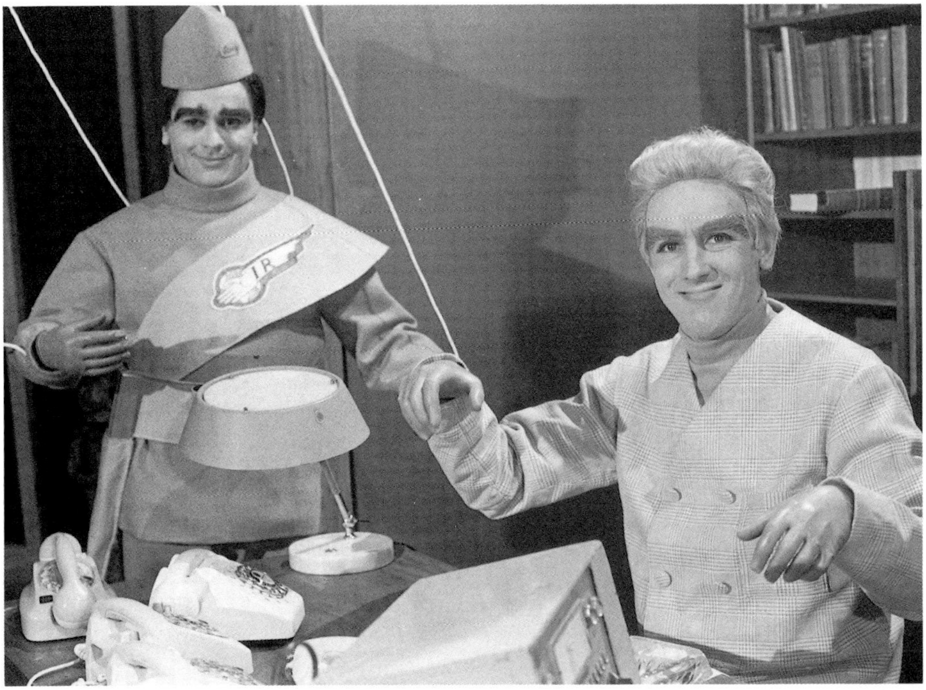

Top: Venus, Steve Zodiac and space pet, Zoony, from *Fireball XL5*. *Above right*: The Stingray craft. *Above left*: The handsome Captain Scarlet. *Right*: A scene from *Four Feather Falls* with Bartender and Grandpa Twink, 1960.

Above: Marina, our silent heroine from *Stingray*. *Left*: One of our *UFO* girls in the outfit I designed.

Above: Lady Penelope with her grown-up model, as we accept a TV award. *Right*: Coming up-to-date.

The media began to focus on Lady Penelope in 1966, after the launch of the first series, and I often made personal appearances in my dual role as Sylvia Anderson and Lady P, including an appearance on the *Des O'Connor Show.* Des and his scriptwriter, Tony Hawes, were great fans of the show and devised a duet between Lady P and Des, with the puppet pouring tea from her silver teapot, while I sang a special version of the song, 'I Like a Nice Cup of Tea in the Morning'. At that time, Des was more of a stand-up comedian than he is today, but he was always hankering to sing. They allowed him, rather reluctantly, one song per show.

He was also a great practical joker, ringing me late one night pretending to be a police officer, saying that he had my parents in custody in Great Yarmouth. I knew my parents were there and that they had gone to see Des in one of his summer shows; indeed I had suggested to them that they go back stage and say hello. At first I failed to get the connection, until finally I recognized Des's inimitable giggle. For a few frantic minutes, though, he did fool me as I pictured my folks involved in some kind of Bonnie and Clyde heist.

Another famous *Thunderbirds* fan is Adam Faith, pop star turned actor and businessman. It was customary for us to base the puppet characters on real people, but it was only recently that I learned how much Adam would have liked to have become a puppet voice in *Thunderbirds*. He was often used as a role model for some of our mini actors, as is borne out by one of our puppeteers, Mary Turner, in a press interview in September 1968: 'We model the characters roughly on real people. Sylvia might say, "I want someone looking like Adam Faith," for example, and I interpret her ideas.'

Prior to the sixties, Adam Faith had worked as a cutting-room assistant at Elstree, pursuing his singing career by playing gigs at night. After making it as a pop star, he was not content just to concentrate on singing and appeared in several films, including *Beat Girl, Never Let Go, What a Whipper* and *Mix Me a Person.* For Adam, 1966 – the year we made *Thunderbirds Are Go!* – was a particular turning-point in his career. It was then he decided to concentrate on acting and gave up his pop image. He has never regretted this and went on to give fine performances in films like *Stardust* and an unforgettable title role in the television series, *Budgie.*

Adam has often been claimed as part of the south London showbiz mafia, along with Michael Caine, Terence Stamp, Terry O'Neill and tailor *extraordinaire,* Dougie Heyward. When I asked Dougie if he had been a *Thunderbirds* fan, his reply was, 'Wasn't everyone?' Not, apparently, Michael Caine, who claimed to be always too busy to watch television in those days. I am sure he managed to find time later, though, when, on the suggestion of the agent Dennis Selinger, I cast a beautiful, dusky model in *UFO*. Her name, Shakira Baksh, later to become Mrs Michael Caine.

Another fan, Gerald Thomas, director of the *Carry On* films remembers fondly:

> The sixties was my favourite decade: recently married to my wife, Barbara; the birth of three delightful daughters; the *Carry On* films and last, but by no means least, the *Thunderbirds* – jointly created by my dear friend, Sylvia Anderson. Also, I was nearly thirty years younger and have to confess to lusting after Lady Penelope and her super car. Although Sylvia now owns one very similar, I have not yet achieved that goal. I am also very grateful to the *Thunderbirds* for baby-sitting my children but, unfortunately, giving them very expensive tastes.

Dudley Moore and Peter Cooke paid us the compliment of satirizing *Thunderbirds* with their brilliant send-up of Lady Penelope and Parker for their highly successful television show, *Not Only But Also*. We knew that we had arrived when they selected us as their latest victims. The *Thunderbirds* sketch was wicked and hilarious, with Lady P attempting, without success, to direct her cigarette holder to her mouth – in those days, of course, everybody smoked. It proved an accurate observation of the weaknesses and the charm of our mini characters, much kinder than its *Spitting Image* equivalent would be today. In 1990 it was rescreened in BBC2's repeat series, 'The Best of . . .'

Thunderbirds fans today are many and varied: disc jockeys Steve Wright and Bruno Brookes; Rory Bremner targetting us with his Joe 90 impersonation of prime minister, John Major; Russ Abbott, inimitably adopting a *Thunderbirds* scene; Hat Trick Productions with their *Whose Line Is It Anyway?*, often using excerpts from the series. Their producer, Dan Patterson, tells me they are all *Thunderbirds* fans. In fact, hardly a day goes by without a mention of *Thunderbirds* in some form or another. Recently I did some television and radio interviews, promoting the Power Themes LPs – a clever idea from Gary Shoefield, a bright young man in the music business and a keen *Thunderbirds* fan. The albums were reinterpretations of well-known tunes from popular ATV series. I also promoted the latest video releases of the series. Everywhere I met genuine interest and affection for the shows. The highlight of my activities was a radio broadcast to the troops in the Gulf on the eve of the Gulf War, sending them a New Year's message from Lady Penelope and talking about my work with the well-informed Bob Harris from *Old Grey Whistle Test*. It brought home to me the popularity of the shows with a new generation. It is rewarding for me, and must be so too for our original team, to know that our work is still appreciated. In our wildest dreams we could never have anticipated this reaction some twenty-five years after *Thunderbirds* was made. Here's to the next twenty-five.

10

THE CULT GROWS

Despite the fact that *Thunderbirds* was a world-wide success, Lew Grade was criticized by his peers in television for what was called pandering to the North American market by producing US-orientated shows. We were really not appreciated in Britain as makers of good British entertainment that prospered also as export material. But that is exactly what we were. Amazingly, Lew found it difficult to get our shows networked in Britain. Yet we not only had a following at home, but also abroad, and, most importantly, in the much sought after US market. It was really a short-sighted and snobbish attitude that prevailed at the time, and in some ways still does. I am not, of course, decrying much good and serious British programme-making, but entertainment is entertainment regardless of setting and accents. Many people thought we were American film-makers living in Britain and no one could believe that a British company could produce pacey material, equally popular in the United States and overseas markets.

We earned a great deal of money for the United Kingdom, with our programmes selling to ninety-eight territories throughout the world. The combination of Lew's dynamic salesmanship and our programme-making with the new technique of Supermarionation was a winning one and Lew's receipt of the Queen's Award for Exports in 1967 was in appreciation of this. It has to be said that our timing was right too. The sixties, as I have said, offered us all opportunities that would have been impossible a decade earlier.

As far as American and British shows are concerned, I think it is quite irrelevant where the programmes are conceived: if they are good they will transcend any social and cultural barriers. Happily, there is now a great deal of cross-fertilization between the United States and the United Kingdom, which can be beneficial. Popular American series, and, in particular, good American soaps like *LA Law, Hill Street Blues, Cagney and Lacey, Thirtysomething,* cannot be criticized for being too American: they are a slice of American life and as such are brilliantly executed. Similarly, British series such as *Only Fools and Horses, Butterflies* and *Bread* typify the British way of life in various social strata – London, suburbia and Liverpool – rather than Los Angeles, New York, Dallas and Boston. The high standards of these shows give us the best of both worlds.

Thunderbirds and other Supermarionation series paved the way for the 'kidult' shows, like *The Muppets* and *Sesame Street,* that embraced the whole family. No one complained that they were too American, and if they did, there was no British equivalent in quality and entertainment to equal them. Of course our puppet shows were over dramatic, inhibited by the limited puppet action and over the top with special visual effects and explosions, but the same could easily have applied to *Star Wars* a decade later. Although they were not using puppets, they did have melodramatic situations and talking robots. Yet there was no criticism then of the larger-than-life situations, criticism that was levelled at us. It is true that our programmes were hard to categorize, and, in fact, we created our own category. Our work on Supermarionation in the sixties became the forerunner to the sci-fi adventures of the seventies, eighties and nineties.

Now, some twenty five years later, we are known as cult and with the reissue of the programmes and videos are set to enjoy a revival. I would like to hope that the programmes are reviewed in the light of the circumstances, and the era and spirit in which they were made. As good, all-round family fun, we were second to none and continue to be so even today. I feel I am able to say this now, whereas I could not say it then: I am more detached from the show by time and events, but having reviewed the series and, in particular, *Thunderbirds Are Go!,* I am very proud to have been associated with the programmes. It is encouraging to be thought of as original and innovative in a highly competitive business.

*   *   *

Thunderbirds fans have always been marvellously supportive over the years, never more so than during the five years of the series first run in the mid-sixties. My biggest regret is that I have not kept safe all the innumerable fan letters from that time: somewhere they were lost with many other mementoes. But some I can memorize and, from time to time, I am told stories about the series and how they affected people's lives that warm my heart.

During the making of *Fireball XL5*, I received a letter from a young girl in Texas apparently called Venus. It was the beginning of a long correspondence that continued over several months. The girl wrote fluently and interestingly: she had seen our shows and now had read about Venus – her namesake – starring in a new series. The series was duly transmitted and the letters became even more enthusiastic. I replied to each one, sending signed photographs and details of our activities. But I noted that the letters were becoming more and more urgent and dramatic, taking on a note of hysteria that alarmed me. She claimed she was a prisoner in her home and that she was never allowed out by her family. It was a shock to realize that my letters over the months had probably fuelled an imagination already too colourful. I wrote to her parents explaining the situation and suggesting they take the matter in hand, meantime I would no longer continue the correspondence with their daughter, 'Venus'.

After several months, I received a contrite letter from the girl confessing that her name was not Venus at all and promising that she would not become obsessed by our shows. I wrote back carefully explaining that our correspondence now had to be at an end but wishing her well. I never did hear again, nor did I hear from the 'parents' or any member of the family. I never solved the mystery but it left an odd feeling of having influenced someone's life in a way that was possibly disturbing, and to me this illustrates clearly the power of film and television. It is not that we originate mental problems, but we can certainly incite and inspire them by overstimulating an already confused imagination.

On a lighter note, though, there were many delightful letters from young fans inviting me to tea, as Lady Penelope, and really believing that the characters were real enough to include as their friends. I would be given the time and place to attend, with detailed instructions of how to arrive in one or other of the *Thunderbird* craft, even down to the last detail of what to wear. It was most cheering and called on some ingenious replies in order to maintain the illusion. I looked forward to my fan mail each day and was always amazed by the sincerity and warmth of our young viewers. But they were discerning and highly critical too, as this (shortened) letter from Beverley Schumack, aged fourteen, sent to us in 1965, illustrates:

Dear Sir
I was very surprised after viewing a certain episode of the new puppet series Thunderbirds. *I wondered if Parker had ever heard of how to drive or the Highway Code. You will have the same doubts as I have if you take the trouble to run the film again and when it reaches the part where Parker is driving through the country on his own and he goes to make a certain bend, then stop the film. I think you will see that when Parker took the bend half of the car was on one side of the road and the other half was on the other side of the road, and also you will notice that there are bushes all around Parker and he would have had no chance at all of seeing what was coming the other way. If there did happen to be a real Parker and he took a real bend like that in a real car and there happened to be a real lorry coming the opposite way, I think you would find that Parker would no longer be with us. Apart from Parker's little mistake I think A.P. Films have scored another hit.*

Master Schumack certainly didn't have a problem putting a letter together and spotting our failure to observe the Highway Code. From such an assured young man I would be confident in thinking that he became either a driving instructor, a police inspector or a stockbroker. Parker did get a good talking to for his careless driving.

Another favourite of mine is this letter from Michael Stott, who does not give his age, from Birmingham.

THUNDERBIRDS IS GO!!!
5...4...3...2...1

September 30 (8.05 p.m.)
Dear Gerry and Sylvia
After watching Thunderbirds *for the very first time just over five minutes ago, I just can't wait to express my feelings. The most up-to-date, fantastic, supernatural (Supermarionation), suspense, unbelievable. No more words can explain it. Well, I would just like to say (on behalf of all my friends) thanks, thanks a million for all the hard, but worthwhile work you (and the APF team) have put into this weekly one-hour-26-series programme! [We*

did, in fact, make 32.]

Also while I'm on the subject thank you for Supercar, *also* Fireball XL5, *also the remarkable* Stingray, *not forgetting a series which I thought was very good, called* Four Feather Falls*! All I am waiting for now is next Thursday's episode, or should I say programme of the Tracy family and Lady Penelope in* Thunderbirds. *Well, I would just like to say good luck with* Thunderbirds *and keep up the good work!*

In the early days of *Torchy* and *Twizzle*, there were some lines written in by the children's writer about acorn soup. Joy Laurey, one of our puppeteers, refused to re-enact the lines because of the possible consequences of children trying to make acorn soup. At the time, I thought it was laughable, but, in retrospect, she was quite right. Why be irresponsible enough to write lines of dialogue that could possibly have dire consequences? I think the lines were changed and we all breathed easier.

Equally, I do think children are tougher and more sophisticated than we often give them credit for. In 'Snow White and the Seven Dwarfs', my own children and now my grandchild love the witch. They are both a little scared and a little intrigued, but I have yet to see it having an unhealthy psychological effect on any of them. The bad influence can be more subtle and involve sets of values that, because they are on the screen, are somehow more firmly endorsed. This is where the real caring and responsibility comes in. In our own way we were probably guilty of some stereotyped prejudices in *Thunderbirds*: we had Russian and Oriental spies, pretty girls and good-looking men, but I do not see that as a lasting adverse effect on our young viewers. And, of course, Lady Penelope wore a mink coat, but then this was common in the sixties. Unfortunately, we were not far-seeing enough to anticipate the more recent interest in animal rights. We were limited by the age in which we lived and although we prided ourselves on setting new boundaries, I suppose we were too obsessed with the space age, nuclear power and their consequences to be more aware of green and other more down-to-earth issues.

But *Thunderbirds* could still help in all sorts of extraordinary and unforeseen ways. Once I was approached by a couple at a cocktail party, who told me of the time their son had suffered a severe accident and went into a coma. It was not until they played him a *Thunderbirds* record that he showed signs of consciousness. I have heard similar stories over the years and the gratitude and appreciation shown is far and away the most satisfying and enduring praise for our shows.

Our fans are international, too, as I heard just recently from Paddy Seale, our talented lighting cameraman on *Thunderbirds*. We always had a huge following in Japan and it lives on into the nineties.

In December 1966 the fans really came out in force for the première of *Thunderbirds Are Go!* It was the highlight of the *Thunderbirds* achievements and represented the culmination of all our work: the thirty-two episodes for the television series and now the painstakingly created cinema version. But however much hard work it had seemed, it was all worthwhile as I sat among the glamorous audience and watched – as if for the first time – Supermarionation on the giant screen.

It was a truly wonderful occasion for us all and reflected the efforts of our talented team who had supported me all the way. As the producer of the film, I was able to push ahead with my ideas which were translated so brilliantly by them. No crew could have worked harder or more loyally. I recognized then and I recognize all the more now, so many years later, that it required a really concerted effort, one which is vital as a film unit. Without the co-operation and expertise of my colleagues, my ideas would have stayed in my head instead of appearing on screen.

We had, of course, the advantage of a series behind us, which had enabled us to assess the popularity of the characters and establish exactly what worked and what failed in creating the best of *Thunderbirds* in a movie. There was no question now that Lady P and Parker had played a major role in this cinema epic, but there had to be the right balance of light relief and serious action-adventure.

The streets around the London Pavilion cinema were crowded with first-night filmgoers; our fans were eager to come out in force. It was a Gala Charity première in aid of the Dr Barnardo's Homes and the press descended upon us in the foyer where the puppets formed an oddly assorted backdrop. Lew Grade puffed away on his giant cigar and technicians, artists and contemporary celebrities mingled with autograph-hunters and critics. Never before had the one-third life-size cast of players been fêted in such an extravagant fashion and such a puppet accolade would not happen again until the eighties, with the brilliant Henson muppets.

Gerry and I had taken a suite at the London Hilton and ATV had organized a lavish reception after the première. People flew in from all over the world: buyers from Japan, merchandising people from New York – representing the sales distribution arm of ATV – writers, directors, voice artistes, musicians, as well as close family, turned up to celebrate.

In the film itself, the dream sequence had given me an opportunity to design a stunning outfit for Lady P. It was a dreamy dress of silver lamé with turquoise beading. I wore the life-size version to the première, which I still have and can still wear – give or take a tuck or two. I felt like a real movie star that night: expertly made-up and coiffured, it made a refreshing change from our work uniform of jeans and T-shirt.

Gerry and I were as one that night. We were enjoying our success and played host to our friends and colleagues, determined it would be a night that we would all enjoy and remember. We were not disappointed. The press reviews had been kind and we were all riding high. It seemed a million miles away from our natural habitat of the Slough trading estate and much closer to the Hollywood scene that I had dreamed about as a child. To increase our sense of accomplishment, the distributors, United Artists, were ecstatic about the film. Their only problem was figuring out if it would take more money than Bond or only just as much.

The Band of the Royal Marines played the *Thunderbirds* march on stage, prior to the screening and I watched Barry Gray's proud expression as he heard his brilliant composition being given a splendid military rendition. It was, in fact, the first of many occasions when the *Thunderbirds* march would be played for Royal state visits and military ceremonies.

Everyone, I am sure, has their own special memory of that night, relating to their own particular contribution. At that moment, all the concerns and shooting problems were forgotten and I was pleased for the crew that they were enjoying the fruits of their hard work. My own outstanding memory is of Lew Grade presenting us with the key to our villa in Portugal, as he congratulated us on the success of the film. With camera bulbs flashing, he made the flamboyant gesture, so typical of him. That gift was to provide us with a delightful second home for many years.

The day after the December première, Gerry and I set off on a whistle-stop tour of England to promote the film. We had a marvellously warm reception wherever we went and our fans came out in force. It looked as if *Thunderbirds Are Go!* was going to be yet another runaway success.

11

THE HUMAN FACTOR

As the promotional tour for *Thunderbirds Are Go!* progressed, Lady Penelope attracted more and more attention. This reflected well on me as the press latched on to the angle of a woman producer, who was also the creator and voice of the puppet star. For the first time the spotlight was then turned away from Gerry. He was used to being the centre of attention, although I had been coming gradually to the fore. Despite the fact that on every production Gerry insisted on his name above the title, we were known as a husband-and-wife team, yet now with *Thunderbirds Are Go!*, I was considered newsworthy in my own right. This pleased the publicity department, but Gerry less so. He found it difficult to deal with this new turn of events, although for my part I did not think of myself as competing with him and only of it being our success. I retrospect, I understand better his bruised ego, but at the time it came as a shock to me that he should resent me so bitterly. Unfortunately, there were angry scenes in the privacy of our hotel room and some public sulks at receptions.

The situation was becoming impossible and I made plans to return home before the end of the tour. I got as far as booking a flight for the next plane back to London. This alarmed Gerry and he realized he had gone too far. He begged me to carry on with the tour. He must also have realized that our problems would be made public if he was forced to continue alone. As much as he wanted to be solo centre stage, he was not prepared to face the final round of public appearances without me in my role as Lady Penelope and was astute enough to know that this would harm our image on the tour.

I agreed to carry on but the enthusiasm had left me. We were on an exhausting schedule and I was beginning to feel the effects of the rigorous work programme that had become the pattern over the past ten years and my health was beginning to suffer. In addition, the cinema returns were now coming in and proved disappointing, much to the amazement of all concerned. The distributors were beginning to eat their words. Obviously, we had failed to put across the message that *Thunderbirds Are Go!* was a specially made film for the cinema and not a television compilation. Although we still had our loyal television fans, they remained just that – firmly seated in front of their television screens and not in the cinema. So, from the elation of the première just a short while before, we were now firmly down to earth.

Christmas 1966 came and went and on Boxing Day there was another domestic crisis. Gerry was still nursing his resentments about my public role and the change in the balance of our professional relationship. The change was inevitable: there was no way I could work series after series with Gerry – so heavily involved with the creative production – without getting some media attention. Of course, this was not a new problem between show-business partners. Eventually one or the other will start counting their lines, resulting in bitter resentment and a sense of injustice. It was now happening to us.

I threatened to walk out again and this time I did. Packing a few things, I went to stay with my parents. I had decided that things had gone far enough and I needed time to think and have a little peace. I was still feeling unwell and had had no opportunity to go for a check up. In any case I knew I had to get away from the stress and strain of our partnership.

Once again, Gerry grew full of remorse and wooed me all over again, to which I relented. He took me off to Paris for a romantic New Year's Eve and lavished me with gifts. We became reconciled without ever really solving the underlying problem. In my heart I knew that it was only a matter of time before the old resentments would resurface and I did not really have much hope for our future. I offered to give up my role in the company but that only made things worse as it was felt that would be making our problems public. I seemed to be in a no-win situation. Fate, however, decided to play a part in the next sequence of events: when finally I got around to having that medical check-up, I discovered that I was pregnant. It now made complete sense to me that my fatigue and illness during the tour were a major contribution to our problems. Thus I consoled myself. I wanted to believe it and looked forward to the arrival of the new baby. For the time being this would heal the rift. But it was not to last.

Completion of the *Thunderbirds* series and the two movies by 1968 proved a turning-point for Century 21 both in our group career and in our individual relationships. From starting as a small group of enthusiastic film-makers, who had stumbled into a new type of puppet production, we had become a thriving industry. But outside elements had started to intrude into our ideal world and our extended family now contained some hostile in-laws, as we were soon to discover.

As the success of *Thunderbirds* grew and became known, we also became the focus of attention for the film unions. The implication was that because we were now household names and employed, at any one time, around 100 people, we must be carefully monitored for any exploitation of staff. In fact, we were rather proud of our track record with regard to the team we employed. Having read sociology at university and being naturally interested in the well-being of the people around me, I was always available to listen to any complaints, grievances and personal problems. Despite the hard work, the studio was a fun place to be. With the males outnumbering the girls ten to one, no wonder there were romances and marriages, with their related problems, cropping up all the time. As the female director of the company, it was natural that I would be the one to provide a sympathetic ear.

We now had our new studio, excellent working conditions for our staff and a continuing programme of work. We were proud of that fact in an industry where the majority of technicians were freelance and lived precariously from production to production. This should have been a source of pride and comfort too for the unions who represented their members, but it was not. I was surprised because as a keen unionist myself, I had instigated the formation of a specially created puppeteers branch. Our specialized type of filming had no relevant union department. Far from being anti-union, I considered myself a champion of their cause.

I was all the more indignant then when we received an unexpected joint visit from the heads of the various film unions. They were impolite, hostile and suspicious of what they now perceived to be the well-heeled bosses and their exploited workers. Nothing could have been further from the truth as our original team would testify. But there were a few newcomers to our studio who proved old hands at promoting trouble. I am not adopting a Reds-Under-The-Bed mentality, but I have experienced the tunnel vision of some die-hard unionists who have contributed to the demise of the British film industry. I saw that element the day of the union's visit and I did not like what I saw.

So what was this visit all about? Basically there were two complaints. The first related to our hot and cold running buffet, overseen by our canteen lady, Iris. Apparently there was not enough hot and too much cold food, which was not an unusual complaint from a group of hungry workers intent on refuelling at every possible opportunity. The second complaint was much more serious and fundamental. Because of the inability of the puppets to perform certain movements, which were impossible in a non-human design of that size, we occasionally used what we termed 'human inserts'.

A simple human action, such as lifting up a cup, was not possible for the puppet to enact. To overcome this, we would make up a human hand to match the relevant puppet's and film the action which would then be edited into the scene. We used whoever of the puppeteers was available and suited to the shot. This proved to be a great bone of contention with the unions. Firstly, they claimed that a professional actor should be engaged to provide the various inserts and, secondly, that a make-up artist be employed to paint them. We tried to explain that these inserts were a minute fraction of the programme and as often as possible we had trained the writers to avoid such shots. Obviously, this was not always practical, but we kept it down to a minimum, as much because of the time factor as for any other reason.

I argued our case strongly and won a reprieve, but what concerned me more was the source of these complaints. I later learned that a new member of the team had been in touch with the union and once it had entered our working lives, things were never quite the same again: we had come face to face with the fact that we were no longer a cottage industry.

Gerry and I meanwhile continued to collaborate on more productions after *Thunderbirds*. We made *Captain Scarlet* in 1967, *Joe 90* the same year and *Secret Service* the following year, but by 1969 our Supermarionation days were over and the studio of which we had been so proud was gutted by ATV and closed down for good. We had progressed to the live-action production of *Doppelgänger* and *UFO*.

Why exactly did this happen? It was basically because we had created and produced – almost non-stop – a series a year since 1960, representing 224 programmes. It was not surprising, therefore, that we had run out of steam with this type of production. *Thunderbirds* had been a hard act to follow and future series just paled by comparison. With our increasing involvement in live action, we were no longer concentrating totally on puppet productions and as good as these programmes were, superbly produced in terms of both puppet content and visual effects, they were not inspired in the same way as *Thunderbirds* had been. We were taking a new direction with *UFO:* it was still science fiction, but without the novelty of miniature actors.

The end of an era came with the closure of the studios. It was a sad time but exciting too with the prospect of a future in live-action programming. It was really with a mixture of sadness and relief that we moved on. Nothing stays the same, and we were, after all, following our original intention of making films with real actors. The puppetry had been a successful diversion but now we were on to the main stream. Our cosy, self-made world had begun to lose its sparkle and the new direction gave us new life.

There were now other pressures on us, however, both personally and professionally as we entered a highly competitive and overcrowded market-place. No longer unique in our type of production, we were just one of many film companies producing programmes. This, I think, was a reflected in of our private life: I had become more independent within our relationship and Gerry was no longer in charge of his little empire the way he had been at our Supermarionation studios. John Read had left to set up his own company and there was only Reg Hill, Gerry and myself left of the original five. John had been a calming influence and he was no longer there to balance the executive mix. During the filming of the second series of *UFO* I was also involved in a near fatal car accident and then underwent a second operation for a thyroid disorder. It was, all in all, not a very happy time.

The problems that had started to surface in my relationship with Gerry following the success of *Thunderbirds* and Lady Penelope re-emerged from time to time and in an effort to improve the home situation I took a sabbatical from Century 21 to write and appear in television programmes such as *Call My Bluff*, *Movie Quiz* and *The Petticoat Line*. It was then that I was also involved in the *Russell Harty Show*. I needed space and so did Gerry.

Lew Grade had devised a series for ATV called *The Protectors* with Nyree Dawn Porter and Robert Vaughn. Gerry went off in 1972 with Reg Hill to produce it. For the first time, Gerry and I were not involved on a series together, although I wrote one of the episodes, 'With a Little Help From My Friends'. I enjoyed the break from the day-to-day demands of producing a television series and had the additional benefit of spending more time at home with my family. There had been some serious problems during filming of the first series of *UFO* in 1970 which resulted in a trial separation between Gerry and myself. We reconciled, however, and went on to create *Space 1999*, which we made independently in 1974 under the banner of our new company, Group Three. It attracted some high-profile guest artists, including Joan Collins, and was one of the most expensive series to be made in the United Kingdom. We became very close to our leading stars, Martin Landau and Barbara Bain, who were also husband and wife. For something like eighteen months we worked together on pre-production and actual filming. They were often in our home and I helped them settle in to their first stay in England. They had been cast because of their huge success in *Mission Impossible*. I, personally, would have liked more off-beat actors to give the series a more natural look among the futuristic settings, but I could understand the commercial value of their involvement.

I produced the first series of twenty-four hour episodes and at the end of the filming, in 1975, we gave the usual party for the crew who had been involved. Gerry chose that evening to announce that he had decided we should go our separate ways. I will never know what provoked this outburst, but for me it was the last straw. He could still not accept that I was newsworthy in my own right and shared the limelight with him. He said he wanted to make it alone without me – that he never needed me and did not now.

The day after the party he left for Portugal to arrange for the sale of our villa. Now I was quite determined to end a relationship that had started with much promise, had achieved so much success and was disintegrating into such an emotional minefield. We separated a few weeks later – this time for good.

Gerry went on to make a second series of *Space 1999*, under the watchful eye of ATV and with an American producer. At first all went well and Gerry lost no time in converting my office at the studio into a private bathroom for himself. It was done with such haste and such efficiency that I realized I was rapidly becoming erased from the scene as I had seen others erased so many times before. With hindsight, I might have fought harder for my rightful place in the production plans of the future. Certainly today I would not have walked away from my thriving career.

Gerry had kept the family Rolls-Royce, had moved into a luxury flat and had the series to give him the prestige that automatically went with it. I waited in vain for some word from our leading stars – some note of consolation – but nothing happened. Such is the way of their fragile world that I was no longer a viable proposition.

It was a difficult time and most of my energies went to limit the damage that had been caused by the breakup, particularly to our young son, Andy, who stayed with me. There was no financial security either from revenues of our Supermarionation series. In the early seventies, Gerry had sold the rights that we had retained after the ATV take-over, when we were involved a property deal that went wrong. As a result, neither one of us receive any royalties for the hundreds of hours of programming that we made in Supermarionation. However, we cannot complain about our treatment while we were making the shows. Lew Grade looked after us well; we just made the mistake of overreaching ourselves and not sticking to the business we knew best.

AFTERWORD

Gerry and I were divorced in 1981 – a sad end to our long-term marriage and creative partnership. Gerry remarried soon after to one of the secretaries we had employed during the making of *Space 1999*.

Today, I have happily found a new career with my writing – which has always been my first love – and my work with HBO the leading US cable company. I am their UK Representative for Original Programming and try to encourage an American interest in the United Kingdom in many entertainment areas. Michael Fuchs, the Head of HBO, is a widely respected and powerful executive – I call him my Lew Grade of the nineties. I count Michael among my small circle of true friends. I like his dry sense of humour and his ability to send himself up – his loyalty to his friends and his keen sense of justice. I owe much to Michael for my second career and survival.

I am based at Pinewood Studios among friends and associates that I have known throughout my working life. After all, we filmed *UFO*, *Space 1999* and *Doppelgänger* here. I have found real and genuine people in my solo career and would like to give a special word of thanks to Cyril Howard who runs the studio and has been a great supporter during my second career. Another good friend at the studios is Gerald Thomas, director of the phenomenally successful *Carry On* films.

I achieved an old ambition to write a novel which was published in 1983. *Love & Hisses* is the story of a sixties' child, living and loving as a woman in the seventies, which I am developing for American television.

Our son, Gerry jun. (Andy), born at the height of the *Thunderbirds* success is now twenty-four years old and a final-year medical student at the Royal London Hospital. He has been my great friend and strength over the years. It was he who encouraged me to write this book as a legacy to him and my family for the work I have done over the years. He and my daughter, Jacqueline Dee, are my great joys and she has a lovely, bright little girl of three named Cyd (after my father with the feminine spelling). Jacqueline is married to a staff director at the National Theatre and is an accomplished actress and singer, so the show-business tradition carries on with their activities.

My big regret is that my sister Betty did not live to share these reminiscences with me, but her influence, her kindness, her support stay with me still. She also did her utmost to repair our marriage in the final parting, even though she was then in the initial stages of cancer. She was a dear sister and a loyal friend who supported me materially and emotionally despite her own desperate health problems. I miss her greatly.

My parents, now in their youthful eighties, continue to give me the love and support they always have. So while I may have missed out materially, I have more than made up for it with the love and real friendship over the years. In the end, that is all there is!

THUNDERBIRDS: THE EPISODES

1 TRAPPED IN THE SKY:

International Rescue are called in to save an airliner with a bomb on board. The Hood is trying to infiltrate the top secret International Rescue operation but does not succeed, thanks to their daring plan. *Director:* Alan Pattillo; *Screenwriters:* Gerry and Sylvia Anderson

COMMENT: As the first script in the series there is a great deal of establishing of the characters and conveying to the audience their inter-relationships. The International Rescue adventure is provided by an airliner in distress and the introduction of Lady Penelope and Parker in the first episode is brief but effective.

2 PIT OF PERIL:

The Sidewinder, an army transport vehicle, runs into trouble while being tested. International Rescue assist with an ingenious plan thought up by Brains. Another successful operation is carried out! *Director:* Desmond Saunders; *Screenwriter:* Alan Fennell

COMMENT: The Sidewinder is another futuristic vehicle designed by the visual-effects department which could well be in use in the 1990s. The theme of dangerous waste which is the basis of the storyline is very much a contemporary problem.

3 CITY OF FIRE:

A woman driver crashes her car in a busy shopping mart. A blazing inferno engulfs the building where a family are trapped. Scott and Virgil execute a daring rescue, before the whole complex explodes. *Director:* Alan Pattillo; *Screenwriter:* Alan Fennell

COMMENT: I am struck by the fact that it is a woman driver who is the hapless catalyst (as you can see, the writer is a man!). I remember playing the American female voices but it just didn't occur to me to query the 'female driver' myth. This is a popular disaster story, along the lines of *Towering Inferno.*

4 SUN PROBE:

A space ship is lost and on a collision course with the sun. Brains devises a rescue plan with some newly invented equipment. *Thunderbird 3* saves the probe but not without some hair-raising moments. *Director:* Alan Pattillo; *Screenwriter:* Alan Fennell

COMMENT: Another boys' own adventure, minus Lady P, but this time with a more space-age theme. Too much space and too many machines for my personal taste but, again, cracking special effects.

5 THE UNINVITED:

The Zombites – a lost race – capture Scott when he is forced to land in the desert. Along with a couple of imprisoned archeologists, he makes a daring escape, the evil Zombites are routed and finally their headquarters are destroyed. *Director:* Desmond Saunders; *Screenwriter:* Alan Fennell

COMMENT: Another Alan Fennell comic-strip adventure, this time with a Sahara Desert theme. Good fun but a little too adventurous for our puppet cast; as always good effects.

6 THE MIGHTY ATOM:

A robot rat, called the Mighty Atom, is programmed to take photographs. It's another scheme by the Hood to infiltrate the *Thunderbirds* top secret headquarters. All it does, however, is photograph a screaming Lady Penelope running away from the life-like 'rat'! *Director:* David Lane; *Screenwriter:* Dennis Spooner

COMMENT: This Dennis Spooner adventure contains a weirdly horrific reference to an atomic accident that has echoes of the nuclear nightmare at Chernobyl in 1986. However, the introduction of the Mighty Atom is straining credibility somewhat, even in 1991!

7 THE VAULT OF DEATH:

A time-lock vault, set to remain closed for two years, has trapped a Bank of England employee. As the air decreases, International Rescue start to burn their way in, in an effort to save him. With little time to spare, Penelope and Parker use a simple hairpin to open the vault! *Director:* David Elliott; *Screenwriter:* Dennis Spooner

COMMENT: A mixture here of the old and new technology: an airless vault, programmed to remain locked for two years. Rather an elaborate and preposterous ruse in order to activate another International Rescue adventure. Parker, too, smacks of Minder with his hairpin routine.

8 OPERATION CRASH DIVE:

Mysteriously, two giant airliners have crashed in the sea. International Rescue are called in to save the pilot of the second crash, but are still puzzled by the circumstances. They follow a third flight and locate the cause of the trouble – a saboteur is hidden in the wing. Gordon comes to the rescue and the airliner is saved. *Director:* Desmond Saunders; *Screenwriter:* Martin Crump

COMMENT: An exciting air drama with excellent visual effects.

9 MOVE AND YOU'RE DEAD:

Alan Tracy and Grandma are stranded on a bridge, connected to an ultrasonic device which will trigger a bomb if they move. Brains is able to disable the bomb and the two are rescued. Scott finds the culprit and retrieves Alan's stolen racing car. *Director:* Alan Pattillo; *Screenwriter:* Alan Pattillo

COMMENT: An exciting and unusual action adventure story from Alan Pattillo. The inclusion of Grandma and the flash-back device gives the story an unusual twist.

10 MARTIAN INVASION:

The photodetector in *Thunderbird 1* is immobilized by the Hood. Once more, he is plotting to photograph the secret International Rescue craft. Scott goes to the rescue of some actors during the filming of a space movie. But once more the Hood's dastardly plan is detected and the photographic evidence is destroyed. *Director:* David Elliott; *Screenwriter:* Alan Fennell

COMMENT: A rather elaborate caper with the Hood bungling his attempt to infiltrate International Rescue. An unusual reference to Kyrano who was established in the first episode as the half-brother of the Hood (and the weakness in the International Rescue team). Another comic-strip action-adventure from Alan Fennell.

11 BRINK OF DISASTER:

Jeff Tracy, Brains and TinTin go on a monorail journey. But disaster looms when the faulty track causes the monorail to crash. *Thunderbirds 1* and *2* are summoned to effect a rescue and the guilty parties are brought to justice. *Director:* David Lane; *Screenwriter:* Alan Fennell

COMMENT: An underlying moral theme to this story that could well apply to the uncaring and greedy 1990s, some twenty-five years after this episode was made. Lady Penelope and Parker justify their existence in this episode by exposing greedy Grafton – or at least Parker does through his past underworld connections.

12 THE PERILS OF PENELOPE:

Lady Penelope is kidnapped when she is investigating the mysterious disappearance of a well known scientist. Lady Penelope is tied on the track of an oncoming train in order to force the kidnapped scientist to reveal his secrets. But before he is put to the test, Virgil and Gordon save Penelope just in the nick of time. *Directors:* Alan Pattillo and Desmond Saunders; *Screenwriter:* Alan Pattillo

COMMENT: This is the Pearl White drama I mentioned on page 66. Alan Pattillo goes to town with this episode and just about keeps the futuristic flavour with sea water converted into fuel! This is *Murder on the Orient Express* mono-rail style and there is plenty of action and dramatic situations, with lashings of Lady P and Parker at their very best. Very much 'Er Ladyship's cuppa tea!

13 TERROR IN NEW YORK:

The Empire State Building is being moved to a new site, but a television reporter and cameraman, watching the operation, are trapped as the building collapses. Brains works out that they can be rescued from an underground water network. *Thunderbird 4* is launched as a huge tidal wave is about to engulf them. The men are saved – but only just! *Directors:* David Lane and David Elliott; *Screenwriter:* Alan Fennell

COMMENT: Derek Meddings reminded me when we met recently that this episode was based on a true event. It is an exciting drama with an ingenious plot and stunning visual effects. Alan Fennell at his best.

14 END OF THE ROAD:

A friend of Jeff Tracy's is in danger during a hazardous demolition operation. International Rescue are quickly on the scene but must not reveal their identity. The rescue after the Nutomic explosion is successful and the Tracy boys manage not to blow their cover. TinTin has a starring role as the beautiful diversion. *Director:* David Lane; *Screenwriter:* Dennis Spooner

COMMENT: Is there such a thing as Nutomic explosive? No matter, in *Thunderbirds* anything and everything is possible. There is a nice use of TinTin as a sex object! Also a good twist in keeping the identity of the rescuers a secret.

15 A DAY OF DISASTER:

The countdown continues relentlessly as a Martian probe rocket collapses with crew on board. International Rescue must save the men on board before the rocket is destructively launched. Their task is seemingly impossible as the minutes tick by. But finally the crew are rescued and the nose-cone detached before the destruct process begins. *Director:* David Elliott; *Screenwriter:* Dennis Spooner

COMMENT: A nice use of space-age technology here and a change of scenery for Brains when he visits Lady P. It is good to get away from the island sometimes. In the *Thunderbirds* era, space accidents were becoming commonplace. Ours, of course, has a happy ending.

16 THE EDGE OF IMPACT:

An aircraft crashes into a relay station and the control room is in danger of collapse. *Thunderbird 2,* using a capsule, harnesses the men to safety. Once again, only in the nick of time! *Director:* Desmond Saunders; *Screenwriter:* Donald Robertson

COMMENT: TinTin is once again used as a sex object here, as a diversion to keep the secrets of International Rescue intact. It is played in an underwater scene reminiscent of *Stingray*. I wonder how the Red Arrows felt about this episode? Brains once more saves the day with the help of the Tracy boys.

17 DESPERATE INTRUDER:

Brains and TinTin dive into a lake, where they are searching for hidden treasure. The Hood captures Brains in order to find the location of the treasure. Even though he is buried up to his neck in desert, Brains refuses to reveal the secret. But once again, International Rescue save Brains and foil the Hood and his dastardly plan! *Director:* David Lane; *Screenwriter:* Donald Robertson

COMMENT: Brains is the victim this time and Donald Robertson once more features TinTin in a rare sojourn from the island. I think Donald had a soft spot for TinTin and Oriental types! I remember the scene where Brains is buried up to his neck in sand. A great puppet make-up job was involved in producing the parched lips and agonized expression.

18 30 MINUTES BEFORE NOON:

A British agent is trapped with a bomb strapped to his arm, under the guard of a robot. He is in a plutonium storage room. The world will witness a gigantic explosion unless International Rescue can succeed in penetrating the security zone and dismantling the bomb. They succeed but against great odds. *Director:* David Elliott; *Screenwriter:* Alan Fennell

COMMENT: A complicated plot here from the vivid imagination of Alan Fennell. As one newspaper reviewer said, quoting the old Harpo Marx gag: 'A kid of six could understand this. Help! Find me a kid of six!' This was more of a vehicle for live action than for the limited emotions of our puppet cast.

19 THE IMPOSTERS:

Two men posing as International Rescue agents save a man trapped in a well and steal secret papers from an adjacent underground vault. International Rescue is blamed and they are unable to rescue an astronaut in space, until, finally, Lady Penelope clears their name. *Director:* Desmond Saunders; *Screenwriter:* Dennis Spooner

COMMENT: I had a good time playing a Beverly Hills hill-billy in this one. A nice idea from Dennis Saunders to have International Rescue imposters, putting the Tracy boys under investigation. The space age of the sixties is put to good use for this story.

20 THE MAN FROM MI5:

During the investigation of the disappearance of a British agent, Lady Penelope is kidnapped and trapped with a remote controlled bomb. She alerts International Rescue via her radio powder compact. The boys come to her rescue and the villains brought to justice. *Director:* David Lane; *Screenwriter:* Alan Fennell

COMMENT: Alan Fennell must have had television back-up in mind for the *Lady Penelope* publication, when he penned this episode with Lady Penelope in her luxurious setting of the stately home and the Riviera once more in grave danger. In true Bond style, however, she calls for the aid of *Thunderbirds*, using her powder-compact radio. The powder-compact reference does rather date this episode.

21 CRY WOLF:

After there is a false alarm from two boys, their genuine call for help is at first ignored. Then there is evidence that the call is serious – one of the boys' father is under attack from the Hood. International Rescue save the day, with a promise from the boys that they never will 'cry wolf' again! *Director:* David Elliott; *Screenwriter:* Dennis Spooner

COMMENT: Once more the Hood is up to his dastardly hypnosis tricks. This time his victims are the two Australian boys, Tony and Bob, played with great fun by Christine Finn and myself. The Hood is foiled again with a clever idea from Dennis Spooner.

22 DANGER AT OCEAN DEEP:

Pioneer 2 is launched after the disappearance of *Pioneer 1.* The cargo of liquid alsterene destines the ship for a similar fate. There is a mysterious communication blackout but International Rescue finally locate the ship. The radiation proves a real hazard but the crew are finally saved before the big explosion. *Director:* Desmond Saunders; *Screenwriter:* Donald Robertson

COMMENT: 'I name this ship *Ocean Pioneer 2*': I had always wanted to launch a ship and I did just that as the voice of Lady P in this episode. I love the invention of 'liquid alsterene' and 'OD 60' as the two dangerous substances. They sound close enough to a trade name to be convincing. The horrors and danger of radiation are evident even in this sixties story.

23 THE DUCHESS ASSIGNMENT:

The Duchess of Royston, an old friend of Lady Penelope, agrees to loan a valuable painting to an American tycoon. However, she is kidnapped, en route. She contacts Lady Penelope by means of her secret homing device given to her by Penelope. The crooks are caught and the Duchess rescued. *Director:* David Elliott; *Screenwriter:* Martin Crump

COMMENT: It would not be a *Thunderbirds* episode without a rescue and a series of explosions. This is no exception even though the plot is far from futuristic. Ray Barrett did his marvellously camp Duchess of Royston voice, making the recording of this episode quite hilarious. A refreshing approach from new writer Martin Crump.

24 ATTACK OF THE ALLIGATORS:

Four men are trapped in a house by giant alligators. They have accidentally poured an enlarging drug into the river. International Rescue manage to destroy the monsters and prevent any further damage from a lost phial in the water. Gordon saves the day! *Director:* David Lane; *Screenwriter:* Alan Pattillo

COMMENT: My favourite episode that blatantly steals the plot from many a horror movie (or is it the other way round, did they steal our plot?). The subject of my amusing interview with special effects director Derek Meddings, this is an episode I can see again and again!

25 THE CHAM CHAM:

A pop group is being used to broadcast ultrasonic notes which will sabotage

American rockets. The device is called the Cham Cham. Lady Penelope poses as a singer and foils their plan – she sings the transporter rockets to safety aided by *Thunderbird 2*. *Director:* Alan Pattillo; *Screenwriter:* Alan Pattillo

COMMENT: This must share the award with 'Attack of the Alligators' as one of the best episodes in the series. Even though the plot is far fetched, it has charm and because of the lovely Swiss mountain setting, has credibility. It also gave me a chance to sing in my Marlene Dietrich voice as Lady P posing as night-club singer Wanda Lamour.

26 SECURITY HAZARD:

A small stowaway smuggles himself to the International Rescue headquarters, Tracy Island. Jeff Tracy realises he is a security hazard and makes sure he cannot remember his adventure. Was it a dream or did it really happen, the boy asks himself the next day. *Director:* Desmond Saunders; *Screenwriter:* Alan Pattillo

COMMENT: A lightweight but charming story and a refreshing change from the usual hair-raising adventure. Although not one of our outstanding efforts, it gave the special effects team a much deserved rest.

27 ATLANTIC INFERNO:

Scott is left in charge of Tracy Island when Jeff takes a vacation. He successfully sees through a rescue operation when an oil rig is set on fire. Scott is relieved when Jeff returns. *Director:* Desmond Saunders; *Screenwriter:* Alan Fennell

COMMENT: Nice to know that Jeff Tracy does get away from the island sometimes and with Lady P too! Breaking the format is not a bad thing in a television series, but the team are not allowed to manage too well without him. More dazzling effects and explosions in this episode.

28 PATH OF DESTRUCTION:

The Crablogger is a massive machine that cuts down trees and crushes them to a pulp. It goes out of control and demolishes a whole town. International Rescue manage to shut down the reactor before it destroys a dam. *Director:* David Elliott; *Screenwriter:* Donald Robertson

COMMENT: This stands out in my mind as a great special effects episode with the Crablogger – a marvellous vehicle design – crashing its way through the forest. The notion of the machine logging and pulverising trees in its path, releasing the pulp into barrels at the back is ingenious. Once more, the hazards of atomic energy are highlighted, as far back as the sixties.

29 ALIAS MR HACKENBACKER:

Lady Penelope is hosting a fashion show on board a plane. The plane is hijacked and she radios *Thunderbirds* for help. The plane makes a forced landing but all on board are saved. Brains' device has ensured their safety and the villains are brought to justice. *Director:* Desmond Saunders; *Screenwriter:* Alan Pattillo

COMMENT: Brains to the rescue again posing as Mr Hackenbacker and Lady P in her usual elegant haunt – Paris. Alan Pattillo understands her Ladyship well and more exciting visual effects help the story along.

30 LORD PARKER'S 'OLIDAY:

The first town to be lit by solar power is heading for a disaster, the giant reflector crashes . . . Lady Penelope and Parker are there on holiday and call in International Rescue to save the town from burning up with the solar rays that have been unleashed. *Director:* Brian Burgess; *Screenwriter:* Tony Barwick

COMMENT: Although solar heat was a futuristic concept in the days of writing for *Thunderbirds*, Parker continued to play Bingo. An interesting theme provides the team with the usual rescue against the colourful backdrop of the Italian Riviera.

31 RICOCHET:

A faulty rocket which has damaged a pirate television station in space has resulted in near disaster. International Rescue have the task of saving the crew. The space craft finally blows up in the desert. *Director:* Brian Burgess; *Screenwriter:* Tony Barwick

COMMENT: On the face of it, a pirate space station broadcasting pop music is not the usual type of threat for our International Rescue team. But it provides the opportunity for exploiting the space-age era that was novel in the days of *Thunderbirds*.

32 GIVE OR TAKE A MILLION:

A gift to a children's hospital contains a strange Christmas gift – two bank robbers! They have accidentally tripped an alarm and are captured by a young boy who spends Christmas on Tracy Island. *Director:* Desmond Saunders; *Screenwriter:* Alan Pattillo

COMMENT: This is the inevitable Christmas story with a difference, combining an action-packed episode with the charm of a visit to Tracy Island by the lucky child who has won a special prize donated by International Rescue. As usual, Alan Pattillo provides the human touch for the *Thunderbirds* team.

SUPERMARIONATION: THE CREDITS

The following is a full list of Sylvia Anderson's credits and involvement in Supermarionation.

FOUR FEATHER FALLS

Book of children's stories published by Collins; scripts.

SUPERCAR

Book of children's stories on which series was based; scripts; the voices of Jimmy/Princess Caroline/other guest voices.

FIREBALL XL5

Co-created series; wrote first episode, 'Planet 46'; script edited series; the voices of Venus/other guest voices.

STINGRAY

Co-created series; created all characters; co-wrote first episode, 'Stingray' and last episode, 'Aquanaut of the Year'.

THUNDERBIRDS

Co-created series; co-wrote first episode, 'Trapped in the Sky'; character visualization; the voices of Lady Penelope/other guest voices.

CAPTAIN SCARLET

Co-created series; co-wrote first episode, 'The Mysterons'; the voices of Melody Angel/other guest voices.

JOE 90

Co-created series; co-wrote first episode, 'The Most Special Agent' and 'Mission X14', 'See You Down There', 'Test Flight', 'Attack of the Tiger', 'The Birthday'; the voices of Mrs Harris (housekeeper)/other female voices.

SECRET SERVICE

Co-created series; co-wrote first episode, 'A Case for the Bishop'; the voices of Mrs Appleby/other guest voices.

SUPERMARIONATION FOR THE CINEMA

Produced and co-wrote: *Thunderbirds Are Go!* and *Thunderbird Six.*

LIVE-ACTION

DOPPELGÄNGER

Produced and co-created; co-wrote screenplay.

UFO

Co-created series; co-wrote first episode, 'Identified'; costume design and casting.

THE PROTECTORS

Wrote episode, 'With a Little Help From My Friends'.

SPACE 1999

Co-created series; produced first series (24 x 60 minute episodes).

INDEX